Volume

1

AIKI GOSHIN HO

合気護身法

The techniques in this book are being demonstrated for educational purposes only. Before beginning any kind of martial arts program or physical exercise, seek the approval of one's physician. The author assumes no responsibility for use or misuse of the information contained within this book resulting in physical or mental injury. Martial arts are inherently dangerous and one could sustain both minor & serious injuries from their practice. Find a qualified instructor.

AIKI GOSHIN HO

Self Protection by Joining Energy

*A Special Thanks to My Students Who
Helped with This Book
Jorge Varela
John Berry
Justin and Grace Clum*

© 2009 Dr. James Clum
ISBN 978-0-557-25638-9

Table of Contents

Chapter

1

The Development of Aikijutsu

The Meaning

Aiki Goshin Ho means self defense methods that are based on blending with another person's energy. Aiki Goshin Ho is a form of Aikijutsu that does not conflict with force or aggression, but rather redirects the energy of an attack by blending with the opponent's movements naturally. The emphasis is on neutralizing attacks, subduing the attacker and restraining him from further aggressive threats. Aiki refers to harmonizing with the attacker's energy.

History

(Sokaku Takeda pictured on the right)

Aiki Goshin Ho employs the principles of various martial arts derived primarily from the teachings of the renowned Sokaku Takeda who was the Soke of Daito Ryu. Daito Ryu developed from arresting techniques called Oshikiuchi used by samurai to primarily protect their lords in settings inside as opposed to on battlefields. The systemization of these techniques developed among the Takeda family in the 1600's, but the art is originally credited to Shinra Saburo Minamoto no Yoshimitsu of the 11th Century. Aiki Goshin Ho was developed to encompass the best techniques and methods learned from Daito Ryu based systems. This was done by over 20 years of practice experience in Aikido and Hapkido. Aikido of course was founded by Sokaku Takeda's student Morihei Ueshiba and Hapkido was founded by another of Takeda's student's Yong Sool Choi.

The Methodology

I encourage students to learn a small number of techniques well and apply them to many situations as needed. Practice the techniques as shown and described in this book as closely as possible making sure the form and position of the body is observed. There is no need to be rigid or formal in Aiki Goshin Ho. Neither are attributes that relate to skill. Be relaxed but be precise. Learn each thing well before moving on and don't skip ahead. Constantly, repeat what you have already learned. Humans differ in terms of age, shape, health, intelligence, aptitude skill etc..... Therefore, each individual will discover what is uniquely suitable to his or her needs within this system. Aiki Goshin Ho is a "self-protection method," therefore it must adapt over time to meet the needs of its users.

(top) Morihei Ueshiba founder of Aikido

(bottom) Yong Sool Choi founder of Hapkido

Defining Characteristics

Written here are the characteristics that define the methodology of Aiki Goshin Ho.

1. Distance, angles and timing are the keys to the correct application of martial responses.

2. Strength and speed should not be relied on to overcome attackers because these attributes fail with age.

3. Force is not met directly with force.

4. An attacker's energy, force and momentum are used to his own disadvantage.

5. Movement is generated by the whole body as a unit and not as isolated functioning parts.

6. Relaxation is essential to develop the ability to feel through a connection with the attacker.

7. One movement should flow seamlessly into the next movement.

8. One remains centered and mindful at all times.

9. It is better to master a few techniques than to memorize thousands that cannot be used effectively.

10. Students are encouraged to develop their own solutions to attacks based on applying Aiki Goshin Ho principles and characteristics.

Philosophical Characteristics

The following are concepts which highlight the philosophy of Aiki Goshin Ho.

1. Control rather than defeat the attacker as early as possible.

2. Don't use more force, speed or power than is necessary to get a desired result.

3. This is a means of self-protection and is not a religion or art and as a result one should neither be dogmatic nor pretentious.

4. Learn to achieve results without the use of force.

5. Since one's self-protection is a lifelong process one should not be concerned with making one's skills dependent upon attributes which ultimately fail or decline with age.

6. Nothing will go as planned so have no preconceived ideas.

7. You cannot depend on techniques happening as they were practiced.

8. Expect that the attacker doesn't know your style and will attack you completely differently than you've been trained.

9. Improvisation is important in the development of a martial artist in order react spontaneously in a real situation.

10. The ultimate goal of martial arts is first to protect one's country, community, family and self. Secondly, it is to use what one has learned as a path of self-cultivation resulting in an individual who by being a

Hidari Ai Hanmi

In the picture above both people extend the hands out on the centerline of the body. Notice however that both have their left foot forward. This is called a left same half body posture (hidari ai hanmi). This means that the left side is forward. Only half of the body is exposed to the front and both people are doing the same thing or matching. If both persons switched feet so the right were forward. This would be called a right same half body posture (migi ai hanmi).

Both trainees (budoka) are wearing large pleated pants (hakama). Hakama were worn by a class of warriors (bushi) and retainers (samurai) in Japan (Nihon). Students of traditional Japanese martial arts (budo) typically wear these pants and a jacket (dogi) made of strong fabric for training (keiko). In some martial arts lineages (ryuha), only masters (shihan) or upper level students (yudansha) are permitted to wear hakama. In Aiki Goshin Ho everyone is permitted to wear hakama.

Ettiquette (reiho) is extremely important in traditional Japanese arts (jutsu). Students at the beginning of class typically bow (rei) and put their hands together (gassho) in the direction of the class shrine (shomen). This is done at the beginning and end of class. Sacred syllables (kotodama) may be uttered and students may meditate (mokuso) in order to focus and center one's self for practice. Courtesy is also extended to your teacher (sensei) and training partners by bowing as a greeting or before initiating practice. For instance, if you wish to choose a training partner to practice with you, you might say, "Onegai shimasu" which means "If you please."

Wrist Exericises

Many of the techniques that you will learn in this book involve applying pain to the wrist joint. These exercises serve two functions. First, the wrists need to be stretched so that one develops the flexibility necessary to avoid injury.

Secondly, each of these exercises teach you how to do techniques on yourself. The exercises should feel painful but in another sense pleasant. Try each one before training and learn to do them correctly on yourself so that you will know what you are supposed to do on your training partner.

(First Example) Point the left hand outwards in front of the centerline of your body so that the thumb points down. Your palm should face to out to the left. Grab the left hand with your right hand as shown. Bend the hand at the wrist so that the little finger comes closer to the face. Repeat this a few times. A small circle of wrist rotation should accompany this exercise. Practice

(First Example) Point the left hand downward with the palm facing to the left. The elbow should be up and the upper arm to the outside. Seize your left hand with your right and turn your hand only clockwise. The shoulder, elbow and wrist should not move. Turning the hand creates torsion on the wrists. This should cause pain as you rotate each repetition in small

Chapter

2

Principles

The Principle of Centeredness

Physical centeredness comes from staying in *kamae*. By that I mean, having a structurally sound framework as one moves about. This is dependent upon the *taijutsu* (body mechanics) unique to each individual and their experiences. Ideally one should keep the back erect but relaxed. The feet should be set solidly on the ground with the ability to move freely and swiftly. Mental centeredness comes from confidence in one's abilities and freeing oneself of potential distractions. These factors are important in evading a technique. If one is centered, it is difficult if not impossible to take a technique on a person by normal means. Any phase of a technique can be thwarted by the opponent's centeredness.

Most joint locking a throwing techniques work because the opponent is off balance. This is done in throws turning the pelvis or shoulders and accelerating one part of the body faster than another. In joint locking techniques the hand is often moved away from the axial skeleton to overextend the opponent. How does one prevent this? It is prevented by maintaining one's kamae. By that I mean keeping the shoulders over the legs and be rooted yet agile.

Here is an example of how to evade a technique using this principle. If the opponent were to twist your hand outward in a wrist lock to throw you, what could be done to stop it? Yes, you could try to pull away, but let's say it's too late for that. You can always move your feet under the hand that is being twisted. By getting your feet solidly planted under the joint you will gain a positional advantage making it possible to reverse the technique. In most cases this means bending your knees and finding the direction to get out. This cannot happen if you are tense. Once I had an instructor who put my arm behind my back and pulled me back to break my balance. He told me to get out of it. At first I tried to struggle, but to no avail I could not get out. He encouraged me and told me to completely relax. Once I relaxed he told me to find the angle to move to get free. I did that and got out. This was a very actual meaning is stronger than just meaning to take a person's balance. It literally means to demolish. Sometimes this is referred to as *Happo Kazushi* which means to break the balance in all directions. When trying to unbalance an adversary one seeks to get his shoulders moved and twisted so that they are not level above his feet. Ideally, we want the person to be completely imbalanced in one of the eight directions before ever attempting to throw the person. Here are the eight directions.

The Principle of Connection

This is referred to *Musubi*. Through touch one feels what the opponent will do. Without touch one must rely soley on the eyes which can be deceptive. If one tenses up and uses strength during technique one limits what one can feel. Keep a light touch as you will feel more. With a light touch the muscles can contract with a sudden burst of energy and this gives rise to great speed. If the muscles are tense one must relax them to move and then contract them again to strike or move. The connection I am speaking off is not only tactile. Connection also relates to ones relationship to the ground through posture (kamae). Also the relationship of your center to your partner or opponent's center is a type of connection. These things will be discovered through training.

The Principle of Entering

This is referred to as *Irimi*. In the face of an attack make a bold entry. This is done by getting off the line of attack for safety and then moving past the enemy like a sliding door. One you have entered, become the axis of a rotation that will spiral the attacker around you. This principle is the same in swordsmanship. This requires courage and strong spirit.

The Principle of Flowing

Flowing movement is referred to as *Nagare*. This is an essential principle in the practice of Aikijutsu and arts like it. One movement should flow seamlessly to the next in a relaxed manner. Beginners should slow down and work on making their movements seamless. The tendency is for students to go very fast through parts that are easier for them and feel comfortable and then slow down or stop at other parts where they have difficulties. When one flows in a technique the opponent cannot find you. When you stop the opponent begins to fix a target or plan and you begin to lose control. Blend with the opponent's movements, keep moving and stay relaxed despite what the opponent does.

Chapter

3

Ukemi

Ukemi refers to how one receives an attack with the body. This generally means falling correctly and safely and also doing various rolls. Much of a beginners practice should focus on how to take a fall safely. Without this important skill practice can be cut short by injuries or the new student will simply quit. Falling is a dangerous prospect for most people. As we get older going to the ground and coming up again becomes more awkward. It is important to recapture the natural feeling of going to the ground and coming up without effort or fear as a child would. When we all learn to walk we constantly fall and get back up again. Toddlers make this look easy. You might say that they eventually do this gracefully. Most people feel comfortable standing and laying down. Navigation of the space in between is what becomes a problem.

When doing rolls, it is best to lower the body to a squatting position before rolling. This will cut the distance from a standing position to the ground in half and thereby make the roll safer if not less scary. Always avoid making contact with the shoulder. All rolls should make contact on the back of the shoulder and never the front. In fact, the area over the scapula is most ideal rather than any part of the shoulder. If doing a front roll, one must tuck and roll. Breaking the clavicle or dislocating the shoulder are common injuries while doing the front roll. Therefore it is advised to get professional instruction in rolling and breakfalls before beginning and while practicing any material presented in this book. It is a tendency for students to want to do too much too fast with regards to rolling. It may look easily but it is not for most people.

Breakfalls and rolling are only one aspect of Ukemi. Another aspect is how to be a good Uke (person giving an attack). Most people like being Tori (person receiving attack and generally the person who throws or wins in the engagement). The roles of Tori and Uke are like two sides of the same coin. Both roles are essential in the development of martial skill. Both roles require full mental and physical attention or there is the possibility of injury. Both persons must be conscious of the each

I seem to be landing flat on my back and it hurts.
Your back should have a natural C shaped
curve. As you rock back much of the force
of the throw will be disperse by rocking on
this C shaped curve.

*I am scared of falling backwards. I can't see where
I am going.*
Clear the area carefully so that you have
peace of mind that you are not going to
land on something. Remember to get close
to the ground before rocking back. Getting
50% closer to the ground makes this 50%
safer.

My hands are numb and tingling.
The hands and forearms hit the ground not
just the hands. Dividing the force
dispersion up between these areas may
reduce your problems by half. Your hands
and forearms should not touch the ground
until your shoulder come up back in the
rocking motion.

From the Backwards Breakfall go into the
the Backwards Roll. Do this once you
become proficient at both.

Yoko Nagare Ukemi (Side Flow Breakfall)

<u>Practical Application</u>
Knowing the Side Breakfall allows you to fall safely from a variety of common Judo and Jujitsu throws. If pulled downed to the ground one will not suffer injury.

To begin the Side Break Fall do the following steps:
1. Find an area that is soft like grass or a mat.
2. Make sure the area is free of obstacles or debris that may cause danger.
3. Stand with the feet shoulder width apart.
4. Turn your hips and torso to the left.
5. Lift your right foot off of the ground and keep your right leg straight.
6. Turn your right sole inward and raise your right arm out in front of you to the left.
7. Drop to the ground on your right side in such a way that your right leg and arm hit first.
8. As you hit the ground the total surface area of your right arm and leg should touch the mat where they contact the ground.
9. As you lay on the ground your head should be up with you chin to your chest.
10. Your right arm and be on the ground with your right palm down.
11. Your left hand should make a fist and guard the side of your head.

12. Your right leg is straight on the ground and lying on its outer side.
13. Your right knee is bent and the knee is sticking up.

In this position you are safer from a follow up attack. You may use your bent knee to cover the groin from an attack and your head is well protected by your left hand. A variation of this is to bring both hands to the side of the head. This can be done with or without using the right arm to hit the ground at advanced stages.

Caution
Slapping the ground is commonly done in Jujitsu and Judo practice in which a mat is used in a dojo setting. Getting thrown hard can result in one slamming the hand to the ground during this and other breakfalls. This slapping action occurs inadvertently as a result of the hitting the ground from a throw. The purpose of the slap is to disperse the energy by using the hands, arms and legs rather than hitting the ground with the back for example which might cause serious injury. With that said, it is not recommended as the best way to do a side breakfall. One should attempt to fall smoothly and softly and not slap the hands on the ground just for the sake of having a sharp looking breakfall. Repeated slapping to the ground will cause numbness and tingling to the ulnar and median nerve

after a few minutes or less. It is not recommend that one slap the ground outside the dojo on concrete or wood as this will cause serious injury.

Problems That Frequently Arise

I keep landing on my back.
You should fall in a position that is not on your back or your side but somewhere in between. Falling on your side could injury your arm and ribs and falling on your back could injure your back.

I can't remember which is supposed to be straight my right arm and right leg?
Yes, the right arm and leg are straight when you are falling on your right side. The opposite is true for the other side. Remember to practice both sides.

My hand gets numb from slapping.
The hand shouldn't reach the ground first. The hand, forearm and arm should hit the ground almost simultaneously. Don't reach down with the hand to try and break your fall as this could result in injury to the wrist.

Practice Your Side Breakfalls on both sides.

Zenpo Kaiten

Crouch low and roll like a ball.

Roll from right shoulder across the back to the left hip.

Keep the head from tocuhing and come up.

The word Ukemi literally mean "Receiving Body." Our bodies must be receptive when we've been thrown. This idea extends farther than just simply mechanical actions such as falling and rolling. The idea of being receptive means that we always ready and prepared to move as needed in response to what our attacker does. Many times when people practice they are excited to get their turn to throw their Ukes. Some people unfortunately look at being the Uke or receiver of the throw as being the painful and boring part and would rather if they could just be the Tori or the person who throws. This however is not only the wrong attitude, it is counter productive to getting better at any martial art. Being the Tori and being the Uke are two roles that are essential to being a good martial artist. In real hand to hand combat we cannot only concern ourselves with what we are going to do to the enemy, but we must also consider the enemy's actions and how they can effect us. By doing this we become skilled tacticians. By learning the roles of being a good Tori and Uke we study both sides of the art we are studying. One is as necessary as the other, and to truly grow we need to be good at both.

Practice Everything in This Book on Both Sides

Chapter

4

Ikkyo

The Importance of Ikkyo

Ikkyo is the first technique taught in Aiki Goshin Ho. It means the "First Lesson." This technique is important because the second, third and fourth techniques arise from the first. Also, if one masters Ikkyo then it precludes the need for other techniques in many cases. As the "First Lesson," special care must be taken to practice this continuously before going on to any other techniques. For this reason I have tried to write this book in such a way that Ikkyo was the clearest and longest section of this book.

Katatetori Ikkyo
The First Lesson Response to a Single Hand Grab from the Reverse Posture

Tori and Uke stand in Migi Ai Hanmi. This means the stand with the feet in an "L" arrange with the right foot forward. The upper body is turned to the side. See the picture for details.

Uke steps forward with his left foot and seizes Tori's right wrist with his left hand. Just before contact is made, Tori turns 45 degrees to the left while still maintaining Ai Hanmi.
Tori covers the grabbing hand with his left palm and steps back deeply with his left leg. At the same time the grabbing hand is rotated to a 6:00 position to a 10:00 and Uke steps back with the right leg.

Break the arm here or apply pressure.

Shown here is a common pin. Press the wrist and elbow down.
You may also use your knees to free your hands.

Kosadori Ikkyo
The First Lesson
Response to a Wrist Grab
from the Same Posture

Tori and Uke stand in Migi Gyaku Hanmi.
This means that Tori's right foot is forward
and Uke's left foot is forward.

Uke steps forward with his right foot and
seizes Tori's right wrist with his right hand.
Toris turns 45 degrees to the right and
covers the grabbing hand with his left palm.
Tori then turns his right hand around and
over the top of Uke's right wrist and take
Ikkyo and previously described.
The left palm moves to the elbow.
(One can either enter to the right of Uke's
body (Omote variation) or to the left or
outside of Uke's body (Ura variation). To
do the Omote variation one steps deeply
between Uke's right arm and right side as
Uke is bent over. To do the Ura variation,
Tori must step to the outside of Uke's right
leg, pivot and turn around. This step and
turn is called a tenkan movement and
creates a powerful turning motion of the
hips which is used to throw Uke to the
ground in a spiraling motion.)
Apply the Ikkyo pin as necessary.

Kuden

Move the arm by turning the hips
clockwise.
Moving the hand using arm strength will
fail against a stronger opponent.
Breathe out as you turn your hips.
Grab Uke's tricep muscles pinching his
flesh with the left hand rather than taking
the elbow.
When the Uke is bent over in Ikkyo, he
must be taken to the ground in a pin
otherwise he will come up to hit you.
When holding Uke down, don't use arm
strength.
Straighten the arms let the Uke feel the
weight of your body.
Project the Uke away if there are multiple
attackers.
Apply a kick with the rear leg if necessary.

Uke grabs the wrist.

Step foward placing the palm to raise the elbow and pivot

*Turn with a powerful torque of the hips spinning Uke around you.
From here Uke may be immobilized with a pin.*

From Another View

Drive Uke's elbow to his head.

Bring the arm into this position.
Step forward with the left leg between his
arm and side to take him down.

Ryotetori Ikkyo
The First Lesson
Response to Both Hands
Being Seized

Tori and Uke stand in Migi Ai Hanmi.

Uke steps forward with his left foot and
grabs both of Tori's wrists.
Tori remains centered and extends Ki
through his fingertips.
Tori will step forward and to the left at the
moment he is grabbed.
At the same time he will move his left hand
out to the side and move his right palm
around Uke's right wrist.
Tori will take Ikkyo on Uke's right arm as
before and use a pivot and turn tenkan
movement to take Uke down in a spiraling
motion to the ground.
Tori may immobilize the arm in a variety of
ways.
A pin may be used as shown in the
previous technique.

Kuden
Uke is tying up the use of both of his hands
by holding on.
Uke's attack will likely come from a kick in
this position.

Uke will often try to press firmly to hold you in place, pull, or try to press you into retreating.

Move the hands to the side and keep them away from being lined up with Uke's centerline.

You should already be in motion when Uke grabs so that his feet will not be fixed.

Once Uke stops he will anchor with his feet and his grab will be more solid.

Uke steps forward to seize the wrists.

*Step forward and to the left, put the right hand on
Uke's right hand
and circle the left hand to the outside of Uke's right
forearm.*

*Let the left hand escape and go to the elbow pressing it
to Uke's head.*

Pivot and turn taking Uke to the ground.

You may pin as previously shown.

Katatori Ikkyo
The First Lesson
Response to a Shoulder Grab

Tori and Uke stand facing each other in Hidari Ai Hanmi.

Uke steps forward with his right foot and attempts to seize Tori's left shoulder with his right hand.
Tori responds to the forward motion by stepping back with the left foot deeply.
This causes Uke to overreach.
Tori strikes into the face with the right fist.
This brings Uke's head back.
Tori grabs Uke's hand with the thumb placed on the bones of the back of the hand.
Tori will now suddenly turn his hips to the right which turns over Uke's hand palm up.
Tori will now step deeply into Uke's space by moving his left foot forward in the "V" shaped space created between Uke's right arm and his side.
As you make this step Uke will fall forward or go down to his left knee.
Tori can extend Uke out further face down into Ikkyo by stepping at a 45 degree angle in the direction of Uke's left shoulder.
Then step out to the right at a 45 degree.
These steps are similar to skating.

Tori may finish with a pin as previously shown.

Kuden

As Uke reaches to grab, the strike could end the whole matter.
The strike could also be used a distraction.
By extending Uke forward his balance is weakened.
If Uke is unable to grab you then so much the better.
If Uke is strong, put your right forearm on his and drop your weight into his arm.
When taking Uke's hand away, keep your right elbow pointed at his chest.
Don't use strength to turn over Uke's hand that is grabbing you.
The turning of the hips is much more powerful.
Any resistance by Uke to have the hand removed from the shoulder could be answered by a strike to the neck or the temple with the edge of hand.

Withdraw the left side of the body and strike with right fist.

Drop your weight throw the arm to weaken his grip.

Turn the hips swiftly to the right to turn his hand over.

Step in deeply and take him down with Ikkyo.

Munetsuki Ikkyo
The First Lesson
Response to a Punch to the Chest

Tori and Uke face each other in Hidari Ai Hanmi.

Uke steps forward with his right foot and strikes deeply with a lunge punch to Tori's chest.
The punch could also be at the face or belly.
As the punch come is Tori steps back with his left foot and turns his body to the left to get off line of the attack.
Tori's right hand guides the punch slightly downwards and forwards until the energy of the punch terminates.
Tori will then turn his hips to the right and take Ikkyo on Uke's right arm.
Tori will finish with an immobilization pin or project Uke away in a throw.

Kuden

Tori must make sure to be on the inside of the line of the punch.
This may be accomplished with a short slight step to the right with the right foot.

As Uke's arm is turned over there are opportunities to strike into Uke's side (atemi).
A kick may also be delivered if his head is down.

Tori intercept the punch to his chest.

With a burst of wave like energy bring the arm to this position.

*Keep the hand higher than the shoulder and step
forward taking
Uke to the ground.*

Yokomen Uchi Ikkyo
The First Lesson
Response to a Strike to the Side of the Head

Tori and Uke face each other in Hidari Ai Hanmi.

Uke steps forward and strikes with his right hand towards Tori's left temple.
For practice Uke may use his fist, the blade of his hand, a club, or a knife.
As Uke starts to move forward Tori steps forward and to the right slightly with his right foot to the inside of the arc of the strike.
Tori's left foot will follow.
Both Uke and Tori may turn as a mirror image of each other counterclockwise during the attack.
Tori raises his left forearm inside of the Uke's attacking forearm guiding it downwards but not impeding the integrity of the arc.
Tori brings his right forearm under the Uke's attacking arm.

With a turn of the hips to the right, and a
shift of weight forward to the front leg,
Ikkyo is taken on the arm.
Immobilize the attacker with a pin.

Kuden

If Uke tries to rise you may kick him or
knee him in the face with the rear foot or
knee.
This technique is extremely dangerous in
defense of a knife attack in which an ice-
pick grip is used.
The blocking motion is a counterclockwise
arc and the right hand makes a clockwise
motion to the right and over the Uke's
head while taking the Ikkyo.
Learn to drive Uke's bent elbow over his
head to break his balance.
Always end up with knife.
Ikkyo as always must be taken by a
powerful turn of the hips.
With a knife involved, one cannot struggle
over the blade.
Stay clear of blade and don't focus on it.

Intercept Uke's strike to the temple with the left hand.
Receive Uke's strike to the temple with a circular
motion of the
left forearm.

Use the right forearm from below to sweep Uke's arm
over his head.

Move the hands into position for Ikkyo as you take Uke's balance.

Finish with a pin.

Shomen Uchi Ikkyo
The First Lesson
Response to a Downward Strike to the Forehead

Tori and Uke face each other in Hidari Ai Hanmi.

Uke steps forward with his right foot and strikes downward to the forehead with an open hand strike or fist.
One should also practice with a club, bottle or knife.
While the attacking arm is raised high and has just started coming down, Tori will slide step forward and to the right and bring both arms up to intercept Uke's arm at the wrist and elbow.
Tori will drive the Uke's right elbow over Uke's head and to the right slightly.
This is done as a whole body motion upwards from the ground using the power of the hips and legs.
Use a low kamae (posture) for this.
Take Ikkyo on the arm and finish with a projection throw or a pin.

Kuden

Timing is essential because if you are late, you will miss the opportunity to drive Uke's balance to the rear and will be hit on the head.

If you are late you should at least be able to get off the line of attack by moving to the right.

Also, if Tori is late, he may do the technique as described in Munetsuki Ikkyo. If a weapon is involved it must be taken away.

Uke and Tori face off in Hidari Ai Hanmi

Rush in grabbing the wrist and elbow and drive the arm overhead.

Take Uke down with Ikkyo and pin.

Zenpo Geri Ikkyo
The First Lesson
Response to a Front Kick

Tori and Uke stand facing each other in
Hidari Ai Hanmi.

Uke steps forward and delivers a right front
kick to Tori's midsection.
Tori shifts to his right by a short slide step
first with the right foot followed by the left.
As the kick comes in Tori catches the foot
from below at the ankle with his left palm.

At the same time Tori will raise his right
hand to immediately intercept Uke's right
wrist.
Swiftly take Ikkyo and finish with a
projection of Uke to his rear left quadrant
or take him down to the ground with a pin.

Kuden

It is most important to catch the timing of
the kick.
The kick makes contact by glancing by
Tori's left side at the hip.
Tori's left side is turned away as he steps
back with the left leg.
This has the effect of overextending Uke
while he is kicking.
Uke may also try to punch immediately
after throwing the kick and so either way
the right hand is intercepted.
Uke's leg is let down at about the same
time as Tori intercepts the right hand.
This creates a distraction to Uke who is
unable to respond to both.
Once Uke's foot is caught he thinks to free
it or hold on.
Before Uke can respond effectively, take
Ikkyo.

Begin in Ai Hanmi.

Shift to the right, catch the kick and intercept Uke's right hand.

Take Uke down with Ikkyo.

Yoko Geri Ikkyo
The First Lesson
Response to a Side Kick

Tori and Uke face each other in Hidari Ai Hanmi.

Uke steps forward with his right foot and attempts to deliver a right side kick to Tori's mid-section.

As the kick comes in, Tori steps to the left
and forward with his left foot.
This causes the kick to go past Tori's right
side.
At the same time, Uke will sweep Uke's
right arm out to the side from below.
Tori draws Uke's balance out towards his
rear right quadrant.
Tori uses only his left hand and arm to turn
over Uke's arm.
Tori seizes Uke's right hand with his right
hand and applies Ikkyo.
Tori may pivot and turn with a tenkan
movement taking Uke to the ground.
Immobilize Uke with a pin.

Kuden

This is a very advanced technique because
it requires a expert sense of distance, angles
and timing.
This technique requires subtlety.
Brush by the outside of the kick by moving
forward and to the left.
You only need to avoid the kick and not
block it.
If you want to block do not interrupt the
forward flow of his kick.
Let the kick pass by freely.
Discover the nuances within this technique.
Examine the pictures carefully.

Tori and Uke stand in Hidari Ai Hanmi.

Uke steps forward and kicks with a right side kick.

Move to the left and draw his arm out to the side with light contact.

A close up of what is happening.

Uke's arm turns over when Tori pivots and turns taking Ikkyo.

Uke is brought to the ground in a spiraling motion.

Mawashi Geri Ikkyo
The First Lesson
Response to a Round Kick

Tori and Uke face each other in Hidari Ai Hanmi

Uke steps forward and attempts to kick Tori's mid-section using the top of his foot with a round kick.
Tori will step forward and to the right with his right leg to inside the arc of the kick.
The body will follow as Tori slides into this space.
At the same time, Tori will gather up the incoming kick in the bend of his elbow and turn his hips to the right.
This immediately diffuses any impact of the kick and upsets Uke's balance by overturning his hips.
Tori keeps his right hand up to intercept Uke's right wrist.
Tori then takes Ikkyo on Uke's right arm and continues with the Omote variation (directly into Uke's front side).
Finish with a projection throw or a pin as desired.

Kuden

This is also an advanced technique that
requires that Tori match the timing and
speed of Uke's kick.
Failure to do this will result in a devastating
kick landing on the arm.
The turning of the hips if strong enough
can send Uke face down.
If that happens one may not be able to the
grab the hand.
Also, if the hand is seized and one turns the
hips strongly, Uke will be sent face down
and will fall badly.
Be careful in practice as this is a difficult
fall to take safely.

*The Uke attacks with a right Mawashi Geri and Tori
seizes his wrist.*

Drive the elbow forward and take Ikkyo.

Step forward into Uke to take him down.

Chapter

5

二教

Nikkyo

When one does Ikkyo it could be interpreted as either a momentary hold by pressing the adversary's arm down or by breaking it with a snap. Since Aikijutsu techniques as they came to us from Takeda were primarily from an art used to arrest assailants indoors, the focus was on restraint and not intentional injury. A higher level of skill was required for a samurai to arrest someone without leaving a mark. Therefore the emphasis is on control and compliance. These techniques must either end in a pin or a projection throw. Nikkyo shows us how to transition to another pin from Ikkyo especially if the Uke tries to resist. Nikkyo is a technique which causes the hand to be twisted painfully in relation to the forearm. The pain is caused by nerve compression due to the radius and ulna being pressed against the carpals. The pain can extend up the forearm into the muscles and joint of the elbow. Applied with increased mass or acceleration may cause the wrist or even elbow to fracture or dislocate. It is recommended that students practice this with caution. It is common that a Uke will drop a knee to the ground as Nikkyo is applied to relieve some of the pain. Failure to do this could result in injury. Be careful.

Katatetori Nikkyo
The Second Lesson
Response to a Wrist Grab

Tori and Uke stand facing each other in Migi Ai Hanmi.

Uke steps forward with his left foot and grabs Tori's right wrist with his left hand. Tori keeps immediately slides over to his right so his body and Ai Hanmi is aligned at a 45 degree angle to the left.

At the same time Tori will cover the back of Uke's grabbing hand with his palm so he may not pull back and easily escape.
Tori will now rotate his right hand over the top of Uke's forearm just below the wrist. Tori then presses downward and forwards causing Uke's wrist and forearm bones to twist painfully into Nikkyo.
Avoid having Uke's arm straight.

Kuden

This technique combines twisting the radius over the ulna in such a way that nerves are compressed causing extreme pain.
The bones at the elbow and wrist are at the end range of motion and any further play in the joint could cause dislocation or fracture. This is a difficult technique for students to learn because there are a few things that must happen for the technique to be effective.

Here are some tips:

1. Keep Uke's wrist and elbow bent.
2. Uke's arm is kept horizontal.
3. Uke's wrist in bent vertically towards Uke's head.
4. Hold the hand just above the wrist with the right hand.

5. Compress the joint by forcing Uke's forearm and hand is different directions.

6. Keep Uke's hand lined up with his centerline and your centerline.

7. Bend at the waist and knees to apply pressure through his joints.

8. Hold Uke firmly.

9. Apply force generously but only for a moment.

Uke grabs Tori's right wrist.

Tori drops to one knee to avoid the pain

Easing up on the pain Uke bounces up to attack.
Tori will step behind Uke, pivot and turn to take Uke
down with an
Ura variation similar to Ikkyo but with the wrist
compressed.

Kosadori Nikkyo
The Second Lesson
Response to a Cross Wrist Grab

Tori and Uke face each other in Gyaku
Hanmi. Tori's right side is forward.

Uke steps forward with his right foot and
seizes Tori's right wrist with his right hand.
Tori slide steps to the left and turns 45
degrees to the right as he places his left
palm on the back of Uke's grabbing hand.
Tori then rotates his right hand around
Uke's right forearm just below the wrist.
This is how Nikkyo is applied.
Tori presses forward and down towards
Uke's center.
Uke drops to his knees to relieve the pain.
Tori eases up on the pain for a moment
and Uke bounces up to attack again.
Tori steps behind Uke to the outside,
pivots and turns around.
This is an Ura variation which causes Uke
to spiral around Tori to the ground.

Kuden

Keep the elbow bent as before.
Keep your rotation of the right hand small
and tight.

Your hands should contour around Uke's bones.

You should not have to use strength to do this.

People unfamiliar with this pain and technique may have their wrist suddenly broken because they won't know to relieve the pain by dropping to one knee.

This shows how the hand circles over Uke's wrist. Press forward and down and the pain will be intolerable.

*Notice a straight line at a 45 degree angle is formed
from Tori's arms
through Uke's waist.*

*Maintain the grip on Uke's hand as you take Uke's
elbow.*

Turn to the left and place the right palm on Uke's right hand.
Rotate the left hand around Uke's hand clockwise.

Take the elbow like in Ikkyo.

The wrist is still compressed as one pivots and turns.

Compress the wrist with the elbow to the ground.

Katatori Nikkyo
The Second Lesson
Response to a Shoulder Grab

Tori and Uke stand facing each other in
Hidari Ai Hanmi.

Uke steps forward with his right foot and
attempts to seize Tori's left shoulder with
his right hand.
Tori responds to the forward motion by
stepping back with the left foot deeply.
This causes Uke to overreach.
Tori strikes into the face with the right fist.
This brings Uke's head back.
Tori grabs Uke's hand with the thumb
placed on the bones of the back of the
hand.
Tori turns his hips to the right to turn
Uke's grabbing hand over.
Tori seizes Uke's right wrist with his left
hand.
Uke's wrist is wrenched by torsion in a
wringing motion.
The body may be used to provide mass to
bend the wrist so the hand goes towards
the head.
Downward pressure is also applied to the
wrist using the left arm.

Kuden

Keep Uke's wrist and elbow bent.
Don't let Uke turn either shoulder away
from you.

*Drop your weight through the arm to weaken his grip and
turn the hips to the right.
This alone can put the wrist into a Nikkyo position.*

Uke's arm can also be clamped under the arm as shown here.

Munetsuki Nikkyo
The Second Lesson
Response to a Punch to the Chest

Tori and Uke face each other in Gyaku
Hanmi Hanmi.

Uke steps forward with his right foot and
attempts to punch Tori in the chest.
Slide to the left to get off line and
maintains the same posture but is turned 45
degrees to the right.
Tori's right hand immediately is place on
top of the punching forearm near the wrist.
Tori's left hand delivers a strike to the face
(atemi).
Tori seizes Uke's right wrist with his right
hand and places his left hand in the bend of
Uke's right elbow.
Tori bends the wrist and steps forward with
the right leg behind Uke's right leg to throw
him down.
Maintain the hold on the wrist as Uke falls.
Lift up on the best wrist once Uke is down
and the wrist is again painfully compressed.

Kuden

Throw with a twist of the hips.
The compression on the wrist is what
makes this Nikkyo.
As you throw Uke you may also hit him
with the right elbow as you enter.

*Intercept the punch as you step forward and to the left
like a wave.*

First an Ikkyo is applied.

Slide the left hand to the wrist to begin Nikkyo.

As Uke starts to rise one prepares the Nikkyo hold.

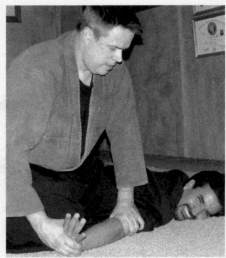

Tori compresses the wrist.
This is a simple Nikkyo pin.

Yokomen Uchi Nikkyo
The Second Lesson
Response to a Strike to the Side of the Head

This technique is performed the same way as Yokomen Uchi Ikkyo. One transitions from Ikkyo to Nikkyo at the end of this technique as the Uke attempts to rise when his arm is pressed down.

Shomen Uchi Nikkyo
The Second Lesson
Response to a Strike to the Forehead

This technique is performed the same way as Shomen Uchi Ikkyo. One transitions from Ikkyo to Nikkyo at the end of this technique as the Uke attempts to rise when his arm is pressed down.

Zenpo Geri Nikkyo
The Second Lesson
Response to a Front Kick

Tori and Uke face each other in HIdari
Shizen Tai.

Uke attempts to kick Tori with a right front
kick to the chest or solar plexus.
Tori steps back as the kick comes in with
the left leg and catches the kick at the left
hip with the left hand.
At the same time Tori intercepts Uke's
right wrist with his right hand.
Tori will come in with the left leg on Uke's
front side like a wave, clamp Uke's arm
under at his armpit and press down.
Apply this variation of Nikkyo.

Kuden

Let the Uke surge forward into the kick so
that he pulls back to recover his balance.
As Uke pulls back come in like a wave.
It's important that Uke feels like he's
making contact with the kick.
The heel placed on the left can cause Uke
to be flung forward when Uke steps.
This is one way to do the technique.
Uke must not have even a moment to try
and recover his balance.

This must happen in a flash.

This Nikkyo comes on very strong and can devastate the wrist.

Remember to keep Uke's little finger on the upside of his turned hand.

The Tori's body weight can cause a break of the arm or wrist to occur easily so care must be taken to prevent serious injury.

The heel is caught near the left hip.

Move to the left and draw his arm out to the side with light contact.

Turn around and apply the Nikkyo.

Mawashi Geri
Nikkyo
The Second Lesson
Response to a Round Kick

Tori and Uke face each other in HIdari
Shizen Tai.

Uke attempts to kick Tori with a right
round kick to the chest or solar plexus.
Tori will step forward and to the right to go
inside the arc of the kick.
At the same time Tori will raise his hand to
intercept Uke's forward right hand.
Tori's left hand will scoop up the incoming
kick in the bend of the elbow.
Tori turns slightly to the left as the kick is
intercepted and disperses the kick's energy.
Tori takes Nikkyo on Uke's right arm and
takes him to the ground.

Kuden

The difference between Ikkyo and Nikkyo
from the moment after what is shown in
the picture below is simple to understand.
Go back and look at Mawashi Geri Ikkyo.
If Uke's hand has the palm facing you as it
is held up, then Ikkyo is done.

If the Tori can place his thumb on the back
of Uke's hand when he grabs the hand then
Nikkyo is done.

In Ikkyo the forearm is seized typically
whereas in Nikkyo the hand is seized in a
vertical position.

Chapter 6

三教

Sankyo

In Sankyo the hand is turned with torsion in relation to the forearm. This compresses the carpal bones and thereby causes a sharp pain in the nerves of the wrist. The hand is twisted to its end range of motion and the elbow and shoulder cannot compensate to relieve the tension or pain. Unlike Nikkyo where the wrist is bent, in Sankyo the hand and forearm are aligned. As mentioned before the hand is internally rotated to cause pain. The Sankyo hold will only be momentary and must be used to control the adversary long enough to set up for a pin or a projection throw. If dealing with one person, a pin is suggested. For multiple assailants projection throws will allow you time get away or put attackers in one another's way.

Katatetori Sankyo
The Third Lesson Response to the Wrist Being Seized

Tori and Uke face each other in Migi Ai Hanmi.

Uke steps forward with his left foot and seizes Tori's right wrist with his left hand. Tori immediately steps forward and to his right with his right foot and strikes Uke in the face with a left fist making his head go back.
Tori seizes Uke's left hand at the wrist and steps forward with his left as he goes under Uke's left arm.
Tori raises the left arm and turns facing the same way as Uke.

Tori can now free his right hand and take
Uke's fingers.
Torsion is applied strongly from the
ground up using the hips to turn.
The force is sent upwards through Uke's
wrist.
Pain is applied..
Tori may now step forward with his left
foot.
Pivot and turn toward Uke as he is now in
front of Uke.
Tori steps back deeply with his right foot
and applies a reverse armbar similar to an
Ikkyo.
Uke falls forward face down.
A Sankyo pin is applied.

Kuden

Uke the twisting of the hips to apply pain
with Sankyo.
Sankyo is a great technique for arresting a
person and restraining them.
When the Sankyo is kept near the chest of
the Tori it will teach Tori to apply pain
using turns of the body.
Avoid using arm strength to do this
technique.
Compress the fingers adequately and wring
the wrist out like a rag.

Step forward and to the right and strike Uke.

Go under the arm and turn around..

Let go with the left hand and extend outwards.

Step in front and turn towards Uke.

Drop to your left knee taking Uke face down to the ground.

Kosadori Sankyo
The Third Lesson
Response to a Cross Wrist Grab

Tori and Uke face each other in Gyaku Hanmi.   Tori's right side is forward.

Uke steps forward with his right foot and seizes Tori's right wrist with his right hand.
Tori grasps Uke's wrist on the grabbing hand so Uke will not escape.
Tori steps forward and to the left with his left foot.
Tori will go under Uke's right arm, pivot and turn around while applying torsion to Uke's wrist.

Tori will try and keep Uke's elbow up, his forearm and wrist straight.
Tori frees his right hand and uses that hand to squeeze Uke's fingers together as if clamped.
Tori will cut down and outward with extension as though Uke's arm were his sword.
Uke will fall forward.
Continue walking forward until Uke is flat and face down on the ground.
Tori places Uke's seized hand so that the palm is on the side of his thigh.
This puts Uke's shoulder into extension.
More pressure is applied by shifting one's hip forward to sending the arm into further extension.

Kuden

Don't stand in front of Uke while doing Sankyo or your Uke will hit you.
Stand to Uke's side.
Some Uke will walk backwards in a circle to relieve the pain and this is not the reaction you want as it means to much rotation.
Get Uke to rise to his toes with lift.

Uke steps forward and grabs Tori's wrist.
Seize his hand and go under the arm. A strike is
optional.

Pivot and turn as you apply torsion to the Uke's wrist.

Continue pressing forward.

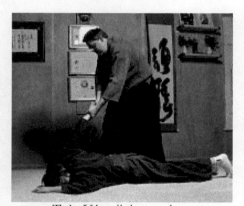

Take Uke all the way down.
Place the Uke's palm against the side of the thigh and shift
your weight forward.

An alternative pin.

Take the edge of Uke's hand with your right hand.

Turn his hand and use the edge of your left forearm to cut across his arm.

It hurts as you cut inward.

For practice purposes, place Uke's hand on his back.

Stand up on the right knee.

Stand up maintaining mindfulness (zanshin).

Ryotetori Sankyo
The Third Lesson
Response to Both Wrists
Being Seized

Tori and Uke face each other in Migi Ai
Hanmi.

Uke steps forward and seizes both wrists.
Tori steps forward and to his left with his
left foot.
As he steps Uke's right arm is raised.
Tori goes under Uke's right arm, pivots and
turns around facing the same direction as
Uke.
Tori's right hand is allowed to go behind
his back.
Tori faces forward and to his left after
turning around.
Tori frees his right hand and proceeds to
take Sankyo on Uke's right hand.

Kuden

Extend Uke out in a forward direction
before taking the Sankyo.

Uke seizes Tori's hands.

Step under Uke's right arm, pivot and turn.
Cut down and out for a projection throw.

An alternative is to take Sankyo with both hands.
Sankyo is applied. Turn the hand and try to get the
forearm more vertical.
Finish as described in other previous techniques.

Katatori Sankyo
The Third Lesson
Response to a Shoulder Grab

Tori and Uke stand facing each other in
Hidari Ai Hanmi.

Uke steps forward with his right foot and attempts to seize Tori's left shoulder with his right hand.

Tori responds to the forward motion by stepping back with his left foot deeply.

This causes Uke to overextend his reach.

Tori strikes into Uke's face with his right fist.

This brings Uke's head back.

Tori grabs the edge of Uke's hand with his fingers while pressing his thumb nail into the bones on the back of Uke's hand.

Tori will suddenly turn his hips to the right which turns Uke's hand palm up.

Tori takes Ikkyo on Uke's right arm by stepping in with his left leg.

Uke is bent over at the waist.

This technically Nikkyo because Uke's right wrist is kept bent and compressed painfully.

If Uke suddenly rises, Tori will take the edge of Uke's right hand with his left hand so that the fingers wrap around the outside of the hand.

The right hand will seize Uke's fingers and compress them with torsion added.

Tori will step forward towards Uke's front side taking him to the ground as he cuts down with Uke's arm as though it were a sword.

This is an Omote variation of Sankyo because Tori enter on Uke's front side.

Kuden

The twisting motion applied by the Sankyo
to the wrist disperses the rising motion of
Uke coming up to try and hit you.
This takes smoothness and good timing.
Keep Uke's elbow forward and his left
should back to prevent an attack.

Withdraw the left side of the body and strike with right fist.
Drop your weight throw the arm to weaken his grip.

Turn the hips swiftly to the right to turn his hand over.

Step in deeply and take his down with Ikkyo first.

As Uke rises take Sankyo.

Munetsuki Sankyo
The Third Lesson
Response to a Chest Punch

Tori and Uke face each other in Gyaku Hanmi.

Uke steps forward with his right foot and attempts to punch Tori in the chest.
Tori slides forward and right to get off line.
Tori intercepts the punch in a wavelike motion from below the arm.
Uke's arm is turned over as if doing Ikkyo and Uke is bent over at the waist.
If Uke rises, Sankyo is applied just as in the previous technique.

Kuden

Catch Uke's bounce up and take Uke's
hand with the left hand.
Keep your distance and extend you arms
outward.

Intercept the arm in a wave like motion

If Uke rises take Sankyo.

As Uke rises, slide the right hand to his hand and seize hsi fingers with the left hand.

Yokomen Uchi Sankyo
The Third Lesson
Response to a Strike to the Side of the Head

This technique is performed the same way as Yokoment Uchi Ikkyo. One transitions from Ikkyo to Sankyo at the end of this technique as the Uke attempts to rise when his arm is pressed down. Mirror Uke's strike so that you strike the left side of his neck first.

Receive Uke's strike to the temple with a circular motion of the left forearm.

Use the right forearm from below to sweep Uke's arm over his head.

Move the hands into position for Ikkyo as you take Uke's balance.

Take Sankyo if Uke rises.

Continue pressing forward and down.
This is the Omote Variation

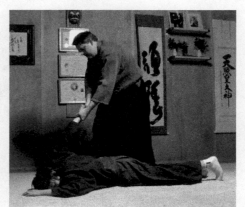

Drive his shoulder to the ground and pin.

If Uke begins to rise, take Sankyo and drivehis arm forward and down.

If Uke rises and stands up straight, take Sankyo with his elbow up and his forearm vertical.

Shomen Uchi Sankyo
The Third Lesson
Response to a Strike to the Forehead

This technique is performed the same way as Shomen Uchi Ikkyo except for the ending in which Sankyo is put on. One transitions from Ikkyo to Sankyo smoothly.

Rush in grabbing the wrist and elbow and drive the arm overhead.

Continue pressing forward and down

Pivot and turn for the Ura variation.

If Uke rises take Sankyo and cut down.

Zenpo Geri Sankyo
The Third Lesson
Response to a Front Kick

Tori and Uke face each other in Migi Gyaku Hanmi.

Uke attempts to kick Tori with his right foot in the chest by stepping forward with his right leg.
Tori steps forward and to the right with his right foot to get off line of the kick and immediately seizes Uke's left hand at the wrist.

Tori goes under Uke's left arm, pivots, turns and Sankyo is applied.

Kuden

Be cautious of Uke's right hand.
One can catch the kick as was shown in the section Zenpo Geri Ikkyo.
I think it is best to avoid the kick all together and take Ikkyo.
I also like throwing Uke forward with a projection throw using Sankyo.

Project Uke's arm out into a throw.

Yoko Geri Sankyo
The Third Lesson
Response to a Side Kick

Tori and Uke face each other in Hidari Ai Hanmi

Uke attempts a side kick to Uke's midsection with his right foot.
Tori steps forward and to the left with his left foot so that his body gets out of the way of the kick.
Tori will seize Uke's right hand at the wrist with his right hand.
Tori pivots and turns to face the same direction as Uke.
Tori takes Sankyo on the right hand using both hands.

Kuden

This requires excellent timing.
If the right hand is closed into a fist, it is best to apply Yonkyo (Lesson 4) which will be taught in the next section.

Mawashi Geri Sankyo
The Third Lesson
Response to a Round Kick

Tori and Uke face each other in Gyaku Hanmi.
Tori's right foot is forward.

Uke attempts to kick Tori in the mid-section with a round kick.
Tori steps forward and to the right to get inside the arc of the kick.
In this technique one will not block the kick and take Sankyo directly on the left hand.

If Uke attempts to get Sankyo on Uke's right hand, it will require that Tori transition from Ikkyo to Sankyo.

Kuden

Whether you take Sankyo on Uke's right hand or left hand depends on a couple of factors.
If Uke's right forearm is more horizontal and his palm is facing me, I would take Sankyo by doing Ikkyo first.
If Uke is holding his right elbow in and has his right fist clenched, I would strike him

first and then take Sankyo on the left hand by going under the arm.

This is how the Sankyo is taken on the right hand if it's opened.

Chapter

7

Yonkyo

Yonkyo is the fourth lesson and the final technique that can be extracted from Ikkyo. Ikkyo is taken when the back of the forearm of Uke is presented with his elbow up. The base of the first metacarpal is used to press into the radial bone and radial nerve a few inches above the wrist. It is best to press forward into the bone and hold the adversary's hand as though you were holding a sword. Hold the index fingers straight. This is not only typical of how Yonkyo is held but also Sankyo as well. It is common to grip with the index finger extended as this extends one's Ki energy through outward.

Katatetori Yonkyo
The Fourth Lesson
Response to the Wrist
Being Grabbed

Tori and Uke face each other in Migi Ai Hanmi.

Uke steps forward with his left foot and seizes Tori's right wrist with his left hand. At the moment Tori is grabbed he bends his knee and raises his hand as shown in the picture.
Uke's elbow is raised up so the forearm becomes more vertical.
Uke uses his index finger to clamp down painfully on Uke's radius bone.
This causes a sharp nerve and bone pain.

Kuden

Learn to do this by using the edge of your
straight index finger against your own
forearm.
The index finger is held straight and in not
bent or curled.
Imagine that you are holding a sword in
your hand.

Raise up under the wrist
taking Yonkyo.

Kosadori Yonkyo
The Fourth Lesson
Response to a Cross Grab

Tori and Uke face each other in Gyaku
Hanmi.

Uke steps forward with his right foot and
grabs Tori's right hand with his right hand.
Tori will rotate his right hand around the
outside of Uke's forearm as he steps
forward and to the right with the right foot.
Tori may strike into Uke's ribs with his left
fist.
Tori uses his left hand to drive Uke's right
elbow towards Uke's head as he takes
Ikkyo on the right arm.
Uke is bent forward at the waist as the
Ikkyo arm bar is put on.
If Uke rises from this position to attack,
Tori will be able to take Sankyo or in this
case Yonkyo on Uke's right arm.

Kuden

If Uke's fist is closed, Sankyo is hard to get. Sankyo is best done on an opened hand so that both hands can be used to apply torsion.

Yonkyo can be done effectively because it won't matter if Uke's hand is opened or closed.
Yonkyo is done by applying pain and pressure to the radial nerve and radius bone.

Tori drives forward and strikes Uke in the ribs.

Keep Uke's elbow up, extend the arms out gripping
Uke's bones like a sword.

Drive Uke's forearm headward
and continue applying pain to the arm.

Ryotetori Yonkyo
The Fourth Lesson
Response to Both Hands
Being Seized

Tori and Uke face each other in Gyaku
Hanmi.

Uke steps forward and seizes both of Uke's
hands.
Tori will keep his elbows close to his body,
bends his knees slightly and raises his right
hand vertically to take Yonkyo on Uke's
left forearm.
The left palm rotates over the top of Uke's
right hand and lowers the hand to the left
hip.
Tori can finish with a Yonkyo pin.

Kuden

As one gets Uke's arm vertical it not only
positions Tori for the Yonkyo, but more
importantly it causes Uke come want to
come forward.
From this position a connection is made
with in terms of a circuit with Uke's left
hip.

Variation 1
Cut down diagonally to Uke's right rear
quadrant as if his forearm were a sword.
This is the Omote variation because one
enters to Uke's front side.

Variation 2
Step with the right foot behind Uke's
forward left foot, pivot and turn around.
As one applies Yonkyo one enters to Uke's
back side.
This is the Ura variation.

Variation 3
In this last variation one steps to the rear as
in Variation 2, but one projects Uke
forward into a throw.
This is a Kokyu (breath) throw.

Variation 4
Take Yonkyo on both of the Uke's wrist at
the same time. Uke will rise to his toes
from the pain. Suddenly draw both of his
hands out to the sides. Uke falls forward.
Use a knee to the face to knock him on his
back.

*Rotate the right hand clockwise until you can position
the index finger on the radius for Yonkyo.*

Step forward and cut down (Omote Version).

Katatori Yonkyo
The Fourth Lesson
Response to a Shoulder Grab

Tori and Uke stand facing each other in
Hidari Ai Hanmi.

Uke steps forward with his right foot and
attempts to seize Tori's left shoulder with
his right hand.
Tori responds to the forward motion by
stepping back with his left foot deeply.
This causes Uke to overextend his reach.
Tori strikes into Uke's face with his right
fist.
This brings Uke's head back.
Tori grabs the edge of Uke's hand with his
fingers while pressing his thumb nail into
the bones on the back of Uke's hand.
Tori will suddenly turn his hips to the right
which turns Uke's hand palm up.
Tori takes Ikkyo on Uke's right arm by
stepping in with his left leg.
Uke is bent over at the waist.
This technically Nikkyo because Uke's right
wrist is kept bent and compressed painfully.
If Uke suddenly rises, Tori will immediately
apply his left index finger to Uke's right
forearm taking Yonkyo.

Tori will step forward towards Uke's front side taking him to the ground as he cuts down with Uke's arm as though it were a sword.
This is an Omote variation of Yonkyo because Tori enter on Uke's front side.

Kuden

This is very similar any many ways to Katatori Sankyo.
This takes smoothness and good timing.
Keep Uke's elbow up and his left should back to prevent an attack.
Imagine a sword extending out from Uke's elbow.
Move the tip of that sword in an imaginary arc that cut down to the ground.
This extension will make the technique work much better.

Withdraw the left side of the body and strike with right fist.

Take his hand, and turn the hips to the right..
This will turn his hand over and put you in an Ikkyo
position.

Step in deeply and take his down with take Yonkyo if
Uke rises.

Munetsuki Yonkyo
The Fourth Lesson
Response to a Chest Punch

Tori and Uke face each other in Gyaku Hanmi.

Uke steps forward with his right foot and attempts to punch Tori in the chest.
Tori slides forward and right to get off line.
Tori intercepts the punch in a wavelike motion from below the arm.
Uke's arm is turned over as if doing Ikkyo and Uke is bent over at the waist.
If Uke rises, Yonkyo is applied just as in the previous technique.

Kuden

Catch Uke's bounce up and take Uke's hand with the left hand.
Keep your distance and extend you arms outward.

Intercept the arm in a wave like motion.

Take Ikkyo on the arm first.

Take Uke down with Yonkyo.

Yokomen Uchi Yonkyo
The Fourth Lesson
Response to a Strike to the Side of the Head

This technique is performed the same way as Yokoment Uchi Ikkyo. One transitions from Ikkyo to Yonkyo at the end of this technique as the Uke attempts to rise when his arm is pressed down. Mirror Uke's strike and his him in the left side of the neck first.

Use the right forearm from below to sweep Uke's arm over his head.

Move the hands into position for Ikkyo as you take Uke's balance.

Take Yonkyo if Uke rises.

Rotate clockwise spinning Uke around you.

Turn clockwise applying Yonkyo.
This spirals Uke around you to the ground with an
Ura variation.

Shomen Uchi Yonkyo
The Fourth Lesson
Response to a Strike to the Forehead

This technique is performed the same way as Shomen Uchi Ikkyo except for the ending in which Sankyo is put on. One transitions from Ikkyo to Yonkyo smoothly.

Rush in grabbing the wrist and elbow and drive the arm overhead.

Move the arm as if taking Ikkyo but once it is down drive foreword with Yonkyo.

Apply Yonkyo as shown here if doing the Omote variation.

Zenpo Geri Yonkyo
The Fourth Lesson
Response to a Front Kick

Tori and Uke face each other in Migi Gyaku Hanmi.

Uke attempts to kick Tori with his right foot in the chest by stepping forward with his right leg.
Tori steps back with his left foot and uses his left hand to catch the bottom of the foot.
Because Tori steps back the distance is too far and Uke's kick falls short.

Tori keeps his right hand up and
immediately intercepts Uke's forward right
hand.
Tori will now move as if to apply Ikkyo but
instead of the left hand going to the elbow
to apply an armbar, Tori will immediately
go after the Yonkyo.

Kuden

One may actually do Ikkyo and then apply
Yonkyo if Uke rises.
In this case one goes after Yonkyo directly
from the beginning.

Step back, catch the kick and keep the right hand up.

Apply Yonkyo right away and take down.

Yoko Geri Yonkyo
The Third Lesson
Response to a Side Kick

Tori and Uke face each other in Hidari Ai Hanmi

Uke attempts a side kick to Uke's midsection with his right foot.
Tori steps forward and to the left with his left foot so that his body gets out of the way of the kick.
Tori will seize Uke's right hand at the wrist with his right hand.

Tori pivots and turns to face the same
direction as Uke.
Tori takes Yonkyo on the right forearm
using his left hand.
The right hand holds Uke's hand firmly.

Kuden

This requires excellent timing.
If the right hand is closed into a fist, it is
best to apply Yonkyo (Lesson 4) which will
be taught in the next section.

Mawashi Geri Yonkyo
The Fourth Lesson
Response to a Round Kick

Tori and Uke face each other in Gyaku
Hanmi.
Tori's right foot is forward.

Uke attempts to kick Tori in the mid-
section with a round kick.
Tori steps forward and to the right to get
inside the arc of the kick.
In this technique one will not block the
kick and take Yonkyo directly on the left
forearm or right forearm depending on
which is more accessible.

If Uke attempts to get Sankyo on Uke's right hand, it will require that Tori transition from Ikkyo to Sankyo.

Kuden

Whether you take Yonkyo on Uke's right forearm or left depends on a couple of factors.
If Uke's right forearm is more horizontal and his palm is facing me, I would take Yonkyo by doing Ikkyo first.
If Uke is holding his right elbow in and has his right fist clenched, I would strike him first and then take Yonkyo on the left forearm.

Chapter

8

小手返

Kotegaeshi

Kotegaeshi literally means reversing the wrist. It is not so much the wrist as the hand that is being reversed. Be sure to put your thumb on the back of Uke's hand around the bones of the third or fourth metacarpals when seizing the hand to do this technique. Press the opponent's knuckles (of the hand) downwards so that his fingers point to the ground. As you take the opponent to the ground the motion is in a vertical arc downward. If this arc is made smaller over time and kept closer to the center it will be very powerful as it will be applied with body mass instead of strength. Don't struggle over the hand. Keep it close to your center and aligned on the centerline of the body. There are many variations to this technique as there are with most techniques.

Katatetori Kotegaeshi
The Wrist Reversal Response to a Single Wrist Grab

Tori and Uke face each other in Migi Ai Hanmi.
Uke steps forward with his left foot and seizes Tori's wrist with his left hand.
Tori immediately steps to the right and raises his opened right palm so that it is front of his chest about ten inches away.

At about the same time Tori will reach under his right hand and seize Uke's hand from below.
As Tori seizes Uke's hand the left thumb is placed on the back of Uke's hand.
Tori frees his hand through a gap created by Uke's thumb and index fingers.
Tori continues to rotate Uke's hand clockwise as he steps with his left foot over his right.
Tori steps again out the right with his right foot.
Uke falls onto his back and the hold is maintained on his wrist.

Kuden

Kotegaeshi literally means a reversal of the wrist.
The wrist is twisted painfully causing the Uke to fall.
The fall occurs as an attempt to save the wrist from being broken.
This is atypical version of Kotegaeshi in that the left hand applies the reversal to the Uke's left hand.
As you will see in the upcoming techniques, the right hand would ordinarily apply a reversal to Uke's left hand.
Tori's movements cause Uke to be taken off balance and also mask the movements of the arms to some degree.
One steps to the right to avoid a possible punch from Uke's right hand.

Tori and Uke face each other in Gyaku Hanmi

*Tori raises his right palm in front of his chest and seizes
Uke's hand from the bottom.*

*Tori rotates his right hand over Uke's wrist putting
his hand in a reversal lock.
Tori can break the wrist or throw Uke onto his back.*

Kosadori Kotegaeshi
The Wrist Reversal
Response to a Cross Grab

Tori and Uke stand in Gyaku Hanmi.

Uke steps forward with his right foot and
seizes Tori's right wrist with his right hand.
At the moment Uke grasps the wrist, Tori
is already stepping back with his right foot
to cause Uke to reach further than he
should.

The left hand covers Uke's grab at the wrist
so that the hand stays committed to the
grab.
The left thumb is placed on the back of
Uke's right hand when it is covered and the
fingers wrap around the wrist.
Tori frees his right hand and rotates it
counterclockwise and he reverses Uke's
right hand with his left.
Tori will use his right palm near the fingers
to press downwards and back towards
Uke's rear and the back of Uke's knuckles.
The wrist is reversed and Uke falls on his
back.
The hold is maintained.

Kuden

This technique teaches the Tori to blend
with the attacker's motion.
One should not wait until Uke can gain a
strong hold before doing the reversal.
The right hand is presented as bait and then
drawn back to overextend Uke.
As Uke is drawn out too far forward, his
natural tendency is to want to pull back.
This motion is caught and Tori rides this
motion in with Kotegaeshi.

Uke does a cross wrist grab.

Tori seizes Uke's hand and turns it over to throw Him with Kotegaeshi.

*Continuing turning the wrist and pressing down until Uke
falls onto his back.*

*Press the shin into the knee joint and continuing
twisting the hand.*

Ryotetori Kotegaeshi
The Wrist Reversal Response to Both Hands Being Seized

Tori and Uke face each other in Shizen Tai.

Uke steps forward and with his right foot and seizes both of Tori's hands.
Tori will his right hand over the top of his left striking the back of Uke's left hand on to the thumb of Uke's own right thumb.
This is done to free Tori's right hand.
At the same time Tori will cross step right over left towards the left.
Tori then circles his left hand over and around the top of Uke's right hand and seizes the hand with the left thumb on the back.
The right hand is already in position to press down on Uke's knuckles with the right hand.
Uke is thrown to his right rear quadrant with Kotegaeshi.

Kuden

As soon as you are grabbed, make a right fist and turn the hand over so the thumb is up.
Striking down must be precise.

You are trying to smash the back of Uke's hand on the protrusion of Uke's knuckle. This is extremely painful if done correctly.

Raise the right hand when Uke grabs.

Strike the right hand down onto Uke's right knuckle.

*Circle the right hand over Uke's right hand and put
a lock on the wrist. Jerk down to break or turn it to
throw.*

Katamune Dori Kotegaeshi
The Wrist Reversal Response to a Chest Grab

In this second section, a chest grab will replace a shoulder grab.

Tori and Uke face each other in Gyaku Hanmi.

Uke steps forward with his right foot and seizes Tori's lapel at the chest with his right hand.
Tori steps back with his right foot and reaches to seize Uke's incoming hand.
Tori will place his left thumb on the back of Uke's right hand.
Tori will then step back with his left foot and throw Uke forward (the direction he's already going) with Kotegaeshi.
Tori follows Uke and pins him.

Kuden

It is best to move back so that Uke must reach to get you.
Seize the hand before he can grab you.

If grabbed, be sure to use the body to make
the throw.
Continue Uke's motion forward to make
the throw.
Uke may be release into a projection.
This is enough to cause Uke to flip in mid-
air.

Uke grabs the lapel with his right hand.

Tori comes up from below the grab with his forearm and takes the grab off.

Continue turning the wrist and pressing down until
Uke
falls onto his back.

Press the shin into the knee joint and continuing twisting the hand.

Munetsuki Kotegaeshi
The Wrist Reversal Response to a Chest Punch

Tori and Uke face each other in Gyaku Hanmi.

Uke steps forward with his right foot and attempts to punch Tori in the chest with his right fist.

Tori will step over with his left foot and
turn to face Uke at 45 degree angle to the
right.
This puts Tori outside of the line of the
attack and still positioned in a left stance
with his hands extended.
Tori will place his left thumb on the back
of Uke's right hand and back with his left
foot to throw Uke with Kotegaeshi.

Kuden

Step back at a 45 degree angle to the left.
This is similar in some ways to the chest
grab technique.
When attacked one may not be able to
readily tell if the Uke is grabbing or
punching.
If Uke is grabbing he may reach and
overextend his reach.
If Uke punches it is best to get completely
off the line of attack as one does in this
technique.
Once a punch reaches the end of its range,
the Uke will pull back the arm.
It is this motion that one will use to do the
Kotegaeshi.

Yokomen Uchi Kotegaeshi
The Wrist Reversal Response to a Strike to the Side of the Head

Tori and Uke face each other in Hidari Ai Hanmi.

Uke steps forward with his right foot and strikes to Tori's left temple with his right hand.
Tori will switch feet meaning that his right side will be forward as he intercepts the incoming strike at the forearm.
Tori will guide the strike downwards towards his own center and to his right hand.
Tori will place his left thumb on the back of Uke's right hand taking Kotegaeshi.
Tori's right hand will turn the hand over pressing the knuckles downwards.
Tori steps to Uke's left side (Tori's right) and drops to his left knee to throw Uke.
Tori may finish with various Kotegaeshi pins.

Kuden

This is typically practiced as an open hand
strike but one should also practice holding
weapons such as a bottle or club.
Tori must be at a distance in which the
strike will fall short and this is achieved by
body positioning.
The strike is not stopped it is simply
redirected.
Uke's strike is a swinging strike and not a
thrust to the temple.
The body drops and one goes to the knee
to create a whipping motion that causes
Uke to flip over his own locked wrist.
Uke should learn how to properly fall in
preparation to be thrown this way.
The average person not knowing how to
fall would have the wrist broken.

Tori intercepts a strike to the temple.

Guide Uke's hand to your center and hold with both hands.

Step back with the left foot as you turn his hand over And press the knuckles down to throw with Kotegaeshi.

Shomen Uchi Kotegaeshi
The Wrist Reversal Response to a Strike to the Forehead

Tori and Uke face each other in Gyaku Hanmi.

Uke steps forward with his right foot and strikes downward to Tori's forehead with his right hand.
Tori immediately steps forward and to the left avoiding the downward strike.
Tori pivots and turns to face the same direction as Uke as his left hand comes down on top of the terminating strike.
At the same time Tori seizes Uke's right hand with his left hand with the thumb placed on the back of Uke's right hand.
Tori continues turning and Uke's spins around facing Tori.
Tori strikes Uke in the face with his right fist and then presses down on Uke's right knuckles with his right hand.
Tori throws Uke to Uke's right rear quadrant.
Tori can now pin as he sees fit.

Kuden

This technique requires that one uses
expert timing and distancing.
It also requires that one keeps moving and
keeps Uke moving.
The Uke must not be allowed to stop or
settle until he hits the ground.
Slide past the Uke and turn bringing him
into a spin.

*As Uke strikes downward step forward to his right side
and turn. Catch his hand from above.*

*As Uke comes around to attack, strike him in the face.
Then turn his right hand and press the knuckles to
take
him down with Kotegaeshi.*

*After Uke has fallen onto his back continue turning his
hand.*

Zenpo Geri Kotegaeshi
The Wrist Reversal Response to a Front Kick

Tori and Uke face each other in Gyaku Hanmi.

Uke steps forward with is his right foot and attempts to kick Tori in the chest with his right foot.
Tori will step forward and to the left with his left foot and pull his right foot behind to get off line of the kick.
Tori will scoop up the kick so that the foot rests in the bend of his right elbow.
Tori immediately seizes Uke's right hand with his left so that the left thumb is placed on the back of the hand.
Tori will now step back with his left leg so that he is down on his left knee.
Uke is thrown onto his back with a caught leg and Kotegaeshi applied on the right hand.

Kuden

One does not press the knuckles in this technique.
A wide counterclockwise arc is made with both hands as one throws Uke down on his back.
Only having one leg to stand on Uke easily loses his balance and falls backwards.

*Catch Uke's front kick in the bend of the right arm.
Then seize his right hand in Kotegaeshi.*

Turn and drop to t he left knee and apply pressure to boththe wrist and the knee joint.

Yoko Geri Kotegaeshi
The Wrist Reversal Response to a Side Kick

Tori and Uke face each other in Gyaku Hanmi.

Uke steps forward with his right foot and attempts to kick Uke in stomach with a right side kick.
Tori will step back with the right foot and then slide back with his left foot.
This is to get out of range of the kick.
Tori will then slide step forward with his left foot to shorten the distance and seize Uke's right hand with his own right hand.

Tori's right thumb is placed on the back of
Uke's right hand.
Tori's left hand is placed in the bend of
Uke's right arm.
Tori steps forward with his right foot and
turn his hips counterclockwise.
Tori applies a lock on the wrist and throws
Uke onto his back.

Kuden

This is what one could call a reverse
Kotegaeshi.
The right hand and not the left throws with
Kotegaeshi.
The right thumb is placed on the back of
Uke's right hand.
One may also throw by dropping to one
knee.

Mawashi Geri Kotegaeshi
The Wrist Reversal Response to a Round Kick

Tori and Uke face each other in Gyaku
Hanmi.

Uke steps forwards with right foot to
deliver a right round kick to Tori's left side
or stomach.
Tori will immediately slide step forward
and to his right to get off line of the kick.
Tori will immediately go a after a
Kotegaeshi on Uke's left hand.

Kuden

If one senses the kick one can intercept the left
hand before the kick even makes it in.
If one deals with the kick, it may be brushed by
or away to the left using the top of the right
arm.
Do not attempt to block the kick with force.
The kick may also be caught at least for a
moment in the bend of the left arm especially if
you are late on your timing.

As soon as Uke attempts to kick step forward and to
theright and seize his left hand in Kotegaeshi.

Chapter

9

四方投げ

Shiho Nage

Shiho Nage means "throwing in all directions." This technique provides a way to turn and manipulate the way an attacker falls. Also it employees sudden changes in direction. This can be particularly useful when faced with multiple attackers because it allows you to put one person in front of another causing the attackers to get in one another's way. As you learn Shiho Nage, pay special attention to how you can turn your opponent's center away in different directions. Notice how stepping and projecting your energy in a particular direction can affect your opponent.

Katatetori Shiho Nage
The Four Directions Throw
Response to the Hand Being Seized

Tori and Uke face each other in Migi Ai Hanmi.

Uke steps forward with his left foot and seizes Tori's right wrist.
There is an Omote (Inner) version and an Ura (Outer) version of this technique.
The Omote variation will be directed in front of the Uke and the Ura variation will be directed behind the Uke.

Omote Variation

As Tori's hand is seized, he will seize Uke's
left wrist and step forward and to the left
with his left foot turning Uke's body so that
his right shoulder is turned away.
Tori will keep Uke's arm fairly straight.
Tori then steps forward with the right foot,
pivots and turns as he does under Uke's left
arm.
Tori is now turned around and will use
both hands gripped around Uke's wrist to
pull Uke down onto his back.
Uke falls on his back with Shiho Nage
applied.
Tori will let go with his right hand and
strike Uke with the side of his hand.

Kuden

Turning Uke's body away from you is
important to protect you from a strike.
Do not raise Uke's arm up.
Slide under Uke's arm so it passes over
your back.
Do not move or adjust your hands more
than is necessary.
Hold Uke's wrist with both hands as
though you were holding a sword and cut
down.
Cut down to the ground diagonal to Uke's
centerline.
Keep Uke's elbow pointing up and the
wrist held firmly down.

Extend your arms to maintain distance.
Use your legs to make the throw.
By bending your knees only you will be
able to drop Uke.
As with other techniques there are many
small variations and subtleties that cannot
be adequately described by words alone.

Ura Variation

As Uke seizes Tori's right wrist, Tori will
seizes Uke's left grabbing hand from the
top with his left hand and step forward and
to the right with his right foot.
Tori will pivot and turn around to Uke's
outside left passing Uke's arm overhead.
Tori will now be facing Uke's rear holding
Uke's wrist as though his forearm were a
sword.
Tori cuts down diagonally throwing Uke to
the ground.

Kuden

In this variation will again turn
counterclockwise but this time to the
outside and not the front side of Uke's
body.
The same points discussed earlier will apply
here.

The Omote Variation

Uke seizes Tori's hand.

Grab Uke's hand and raise up using the forearm to break his fingers.

*Step under the arm, pivot and turn holding
Uke's arm like a sword.*

*Cut down and pin Uke's hand to the ground.
Stand up, back away and maintain
Mindfulness (zanshin)*

Kosadori Shiho Nage
The Four Directions Throw Against a Cross Wrist Grab

Tori and Uke face each other in Gyaku Hanmi.

Uke steps forward with his right foot and seizes Tori's right hand with his right hand. For this technique there is also an Omote and Ura variation.

Omote Variation

The moment Tori is grabbed, he will cover Uke's grabbing hand with his left hand. Tori will step forward with his left foot then his right and then his left again. He'll pivot and turn going under Uke's left arm. Holding Uke's wrist like a sword, Tori will cut down throwing Uke on his back.

Kuden

Taking so many steps causes Uke to be turned around towards his rear and keeps him from attacking you with his other arm.

Uke's arm should be kept straight while stepping and one should extend the arms out in front of you.

Ura Variation

At the moment Uke grabs Uke, Tori will cover the grabbing hand and begin to turn clockwise extending Uke's arm forward. Tori goes under the arm and Shiho Nage is take on Uke's right arm.
Uke is thrown down onto his back.

Kuden

Don't raise Uke's arm and don't turn around in front of him.
Turn until your back is against Uke's right side.
Bend forward and let the arm pass over your back and head staying close to Uke.
Always keep Uke's elbow up.
Extend the arms and cut down.

Uke seizes Tori's wrist with a cross grab.

Tori steps forward, seizes the hand and begins to turn clockwise to the outside.

*Step back with the right foot, draw Uke forward and
then his arm over the head and back.*

*Turn quickly and cut down.
This demonstrates an Ura variation of
Shiho Nage.*

Another possibility is to step out, extend the arms, and bend the knees to drop Uke.

Ryotetori Shiho Nage
The Four Direction Throw Response to Both Hands Being Seized

Tori and Uke face each other in Shizen Tai.

Uke steps forward with his right foot and seizes Tori's wrists.
Tori will seize Uke's left wrist with his left hand.
Tori then turns the outer edge of his right hand horizontally facing Uke.

Tori bends his knees and rises pulling Uke's
left wrist towards himself and pushing
Uke's fingers back.
This is painful.
Tori will then slide the step forward to the
left with his left foot step through with the
right foot so that he turns around and take
Omote Shiho Nage on Uke's left arm.
Uke is thrown to the ground on his back.

Kuden

Use the right forearm to bend the fingers
back.
This will get Uke up on his toes.
Bend your knees and come up from below
and then suddenly turn to do the Shiho
Nage.

*As soon as both hands are seized, grab Uke's left
and raise up.*

Step forward and to the left turning Uke clockwise.

Step, pivot and turn going under the arm. Cut down as though holding a sword.

Katamune Dori Shiho Nage
The Four Directions Throw Response to a Chest Grab

Tori and Uke face each other in Shizen Tai.

Uke steps forward with his right foot and
seizes Tori's lapel with his right hand.
Tori steps back at the same time with his
left foot and seizes Uke's grabbing hand
from below with his right hand.
Tori's right thumb is place on the palm side
of the wrist.
Tori will now move his left shoulder in
under Uke's right elbow as he turns
clockwise.
Tori breaks Uke's elbow as he does this by
leveraging it on his left shoulder.
Tori continues to turn to Uke's outside
applying Ura Shiho Nage.
Uke is thrown down on his back.

Kuden

Presented here is the Ura variation, but one
could also do an Omote variation by
stepping to Uke's front side.

When Uke seizes the lapel, Tori reaches and takes the hand as shown from below.

Turn clockwise bringing your shoulder up under Uke's arm to break the elbow.

Turn around and take Uke down with
Shiho Nage.

Cut down to the ground and hold the hand to
the ground to pin.

Munetsuki Shiho Nage
The Four Direction Throw Response to a Chest Punch

Tori and Uke face each other in Gyaku Hanmi.

Uke steps forward with his right foot and punches to Tori's chest or stomach with his right hand.
Tori will slide step back with both feet to make the punch fall short and overextend Uke's reach.
Tori seizes Uke's right wrist with both hands, steps forward with the left foot and turns around.
Tori will go under Uke's arm and throw with Ura Shiho Nage.

Kuden

If one is not going to get off line of an attack then one must move back to be out of reach.
This is dangerous because a follow up attack from the opponent's other hand is likely.
Catch the fist by using both hands.

The thumb and index fingers will surround
the attacker's wrist as you catch the fist.
An Ura variation is used here to do Shiho
Nage.

Yokomen Uchi Shiho Nage
The Four Directions Throw in Response to a Right Strike to the Side of the Head

Tori and Uke stand in Hidari Ai Hanmi.

Uke steps forward with and strike to the left
side of Tori's head with his right hand.
As the strike come in Tori intercepts the left
hand by redirecting the strike with the edge of
his hand and steps back with the left foot.
Uke's hand is guided to Tori's center.
Tori may either do Omote Shiho Nage or Ura
Shiho Nage.

Kuden

It is important to maintain a distance in which
Uke's strike will not reach the temple.
Also, it is essential that the strike is not
blocked but only directed towards the center.
By the center I mean the centerline in front of
the abdomen.
Make sure Uke does not bend his arm for
either Omote or Ura variations of Shiho
Nage.
When the right hand makes contact with
Uke's hand, use your right thumb to
compress his radial pulse.

*Intercept the strike to the side of the head with
the left hand.*

Guide the hand to the other hand at your center.

Step forward turning Uke's body away from you.

Turn and throw Uke down.

Hold Uke's wrist to the ground and move away.

Shomen Uchi Shiho Nage
The Four Directions Throw Response to a Strike to the Forehead

Tori and Uke face each other in Gyaku Hanmi.

Uke steps forward with this right foot and strikes down to Tori's forehead with his right hand.
Step forward and to the left passing by Uke's right side as he strikes down.
Pivot and turn facing the same direction as Uke.
Seize Uke's right hand from the top and step back with the left foot.
As Uke turns to come at you strike to his face with the right hand.
Change your contact at Uke's wrist and throw Uke with Ura Shiho Nage.

Kuden

Shomen Uchi is not an attack which one can easily use Shiho Nage.
This technique is similar to Shomen Uchi Kotegaeshi as far as its entry is concerned.

Zenpo Geri Shiho Nage
The Four Directions Throw Response to a Front Kick

Tori and Uke face each other in Hidari Ai Hanmi.

Uke steps forward and attempts to kick Tori in the chest or stomach with a front kick.
Tori will step back with the left foot and catch the kick by the heel with the left palm.
The kick is held at the left hip while the right hand sweeps inside Uke's right forearm.
Tori will seizes Uke's right wrist from the inside with the right hand.
Tori then abandons the captured kick and steps forward with his right foot and then his left.
Tori pivots and turns to face the same direction as Uke.
As Tori turns he will go under Uke's right arm on the front side of Uke's body that is now turned to his left.
Tori throws Uke with Omote Shiho Nage.

Kuden

The technique will be easier if Uke's arms happen to be extended a little when he kicks.

Yoko Geri Shiho Nage
The Four Direction Throw Response to a Side Kick

Tori and Uke face each other in Gyaku Hanmi.

Uke steps forward and kicks to Tori's chest or stomach with a right side kick.
Tori slide steps back to avoid the kick and then jumps in and takes Ura Shiho Nage on Uke's right arm.

Kuden

This take superb timing .
If the placement of the hands is confusing to you, think of forming a ring with your thumb and index fingers as you seizes Uke's right wrist.

Mawashi Geri Shiho Nage
The Four Directions Response to a Round Kick

Tori and Uke face each other in Gyaku Hanmi.

Uke steps forward and attempts to kick Tori in the side with a round kick.
Tori enters by stepping forward with the right foot inside the kick and immediately goes after Uke's left hand.
Tori seizes Uke's left hand with both hands and turns around applying Shiho Nage.
Tori cuts down and Uke falls to back.

Kuden

This is an Ura variation of Shiho Nage applied on the left arm.

Uke attacks with a right round kick.

*Tori seizes the wrist, goes under the
arm and turns around.*

Cut down to the ground

呼吸投げ

Kokyu Nage

Kokyu Nage means "breath throw." These throws mimic the expansion and contraction seen in the lungs when we breathe. Breathing is essential to life. It is how we draw in the vital air (Ki) into our bodies. One should keep this in mind while practicing. Rising and falling, entering and exiting, opening and closing may all be experienced within this form.

Katatetori Kokyu Nage
The Breath Throw Response to the Hand Being Grabbed

Tori and Uke face each other in Migi Ai Hanmi.

Uke steps forward with his left foot and seizes Uke's right hand.
As Tori's hand is grabbed he will not offer any resistance and yield to the grab.
Uke's right hand will collapse to his center which allows Uke to come forward.
Tori's right hand will be palm up and he will bend his knees.
Tori moves his right hand in a vertical arc over Uke's head towards his right shoulder.
Tori straightens his legs as he does this and steps behinds Uke's left leg.
Tori will now extend beyond Uke and bring the back of his arm down across Uke's chest.
Uke will fall on his back.

Kuden

When being grabbed by the hand the feeling
is that Tori is breathing in Uke's motion.
When Tori throws he breathes out and the
feeling is like he is throwing with the
exhalation.
Arcs and spirals are used throughout all
techniques in this system.
Kokyu techniques employ a vertical arc that
starts low and then rises over the Uke's head.
Extension is important with this technique as
it is with most techniques.
Extend beyond Uke and you will be more
successful.
Your body particularly your right arm and
shoulder will occupy Uke's space causing him
to fall backwards.
If y6u meet any resistance drop your weight
by bending your knees and apply your weight
downwards through Uke to make him fall.
Problems often arise when Tori attempts to
make a more horizontal arc.
This will alert the Uke and he will resist.
The feeling of the right hand and arm is like a
flower opening.
The left hand being free can strike Uke in the
belly.
The step behind Uke's leg acts as a stumbling
block.
It is essential that Uke is put into a position
where his head is back and his back is arched
to the rear.

Uke seizes Tori's wrist.

Tori yields to the grab and Uke surges forward.

*Raise the hand over Uke's chest and
extend out over his head.*

Uke falls on his back.

Katatori Kokyu Nage Tenkan (Turning) Variation

Uke seizes Tori's hand.

*Tori makes steps and turns with a Tenkan
movement to face the same direction.*

Tori turns his hip clockwise and throws Uke.

Katatetori Kokyu Nage Mae (Front) Variation

Uke seizes Tori's hand.

Tori makes steps and turns with a Tenkan movement to face the same direction

*Tori steps forward and does a projection
throw with Kokyu (breath).*

Kosadori Kokyu Nage
The Breath Throw
Response to a Cross Grab

Tori and Uke stand in Gyaku Hanmi.

Uke steps forward and seizes Tori's right
hand hand at the wrist with his right hand.
Tori will yield to the grab and step forward
with his left foot behind Uke's right foot.
At the same time Tori will turn to his right
bending his knees to lower himself with his
left arm above Uke's arm.
Tori will move the back of his arm in a
vertical arc as he turns his hips to the left.
The arc rises over Uke's chest and head and
extends outward.
This is Kokyu Nage.
Uke falls to his back.

Kuden

This has the feeling of contraction and
expansion.
There is a horizontal component to this
technique due to the rotation of the hips.
This clearly places Tori's arm well into Uke's
space.
This technique, as well as the first one, are
typically practiced statically meaning that there
is not much forward motion or moment in
the attack.
Once the technique is learned statically then
more motion can be applied.
As more motion is applied one sees that
Uke's hips continue to come forward but his
head is suddenly moved back.
This creates problems maintaining balance
and causes the fall.
A person unaware that he should keep his
head back in order to avoid Uke's arm will of
course be hit.
A harsher way of applying this technique is to
actually hit the Uke in the face with the elbow.

Uke seizes Tori's wrist with a cross grab.

Turn the hand and hips to the right to turn Uke's shoulders.

*Step in open the left hand up widely
extending over Uke's chest and head.*

Ryotetori Kokyu Nage
The Breath Throw Response to Both Hands Being Seized

Tori and Uke face each other in Shizen Tai.

Uke steps forward and seizes both of Tori's wrists.
Tori yields to the grabs as Uke presses forward.

Tori will raises his right hand up over the left.
Tori keeps the left hand closer to his left side.
Tori now steps behind Uke's left leg and
throws with Kokyu Nage .
Uke falls to his back.

Kuden

Keep the right hand higher and the left hand
lower.
As before extend your right arm over Uke's
chest to draw his head back.
Always keep the back of the hand and arm
facing Uke.

Uke seizes both of Tori's wrists.

Tori raises his right hand up over his left.

*Tori extends his right hand over Uke's chest
and steps forward behind Uke's left foot.*

Tori bends his knees and extends outward
as he turns his hips to the right.

Ryotetori Kokyu Nage can also be a
projection throw.

Uke grabs Tori's wrists.

*Right step forward and turns around going
under the arm.*

Cut down projecting Uke into a throw.

Katamune Dori
Kokyu Nage
The Breath Throw
Response to a Chest Grab

Tori and Uke face each other in Gyaku
Hanmi.

Uke steps forward and seizes Tori lapel with
his right hand.
Tori steps forward with his left foot and
depending on the distance may step back
slightly with the right foot.
At the same time, will drop his center low by
bending his knees and bring his left arm over
the top of Uke's right.
Tori sinks down low as if to gather energy and
breathes in.
Tori will now open his arms like a flower
opening and extend over Uke's left shoulder.
Tori may step behind Uke's right foot with
his left as he does this but it may not be
necessary to adequately throw Uke.
Tori rotates his hips to the left, and breathes
out to throw with Kokyu Nage.
Uke falls to his back.

Kuden

If one is grabbed by the chest with both
hands, this technique can be applied also.
Keep the back straight and don't bend
forward.
Bend at the knees and not at the waist.

Uke seizes Tori's lapel.

*Tori steps forward and brings his arms down
over Uke's arm.*

*Tori rises and turns his hips couterclockwise
to throw Uke with Kokyu Nage.*

Munetsuki Kokyu Nage
The Breath Throw
Response to a Chest Punch

Tori and Uke face each other in Hidari Ai Hanmi

Uke steps forward with his right foot and punches to Tori's chest or stomach with his right fist.
Uke slides steps slightly offline forward and to the left.

Tori's right hand will guide Uke's right wrist
downward using the web of the hand
between the thumb and index fingers.
The left hand will immediately shoot in across
Uke's face and left shoulder.
Uke will have to move his head back of be
hit.
Once his head moves back far enough he can
no longer keep his balance as his hips are still
accelerating forward.
Uke will fall from Kokyu Nage.

Kuden

The left arm will take the space previously
occupied by Uke's head.
The edge of the forearm (inner or outer side)
may be useed to strike the neck or head.
There is a shearing motion as the right hand
draws in and the left hand extends out.
This is simultaneous defense and offense.
While training, the Uke will learn to move his
head back to avoid being hit.
This is a self-defense skill that must be learned
from Kokyu Nage.

*Move off line and at the same time shoot past
Uke's head and left shoulder with the left hand.*

Yokomen Uchi Kokyu Nage
The Breath Throw Response to a Strike to the Side of the Head

Tori and Uke face each other in Hidari Ai
Hanmi.

Uke steps forward with his right foot, and
strikes to the side of Tori's head with a right
diagonal strike.
Uke comes with a lot of momentum.
Tori sees Uke coming and starts moving to
the right.

This causes Uke to reset his target in motion causing him to begin tracking while still moving.

This example presents a circular attack on a moving target.

This is not a linear attack.

Both Tori and Uke turn within the space facing opposite directions as Tori mirrors Uke's movement.

Tori intercepts the strike and guides it to his center with both hands.

Tori will now step forward with his left foot and pass his left arm over Uke's right arm.

Tori will bend his knees and sink down before rising up, turning his hips and throwing Uke.

Kuden

Representing motion in still frames is a challenge.

One must see this actually demonstrated and this will make better sense.

Since the strike carries a lot of momentum, the strike is diffused by making it continue on its path following in a spiral around.

Intercept the strike to the side of the head with the left hand.

Guide the Yokomen strike to your center.

Step in, turn the hips and throw.

Shomen Uchi Kokyu Nage
The Breath Throw Response to a Strike to the Forehead

Tori and Uke face each other in Gyaku Hanmi.

Uke steps forward with his right foot and attempts to strike Tori on the forehead with a downward strike.

Tori steps forward with his left foot, and forms a triangular shape with both arms creating a wedge that Uke's strike will slide past.
Tori will now turn abruptly and guides Uke's right arm down with the edge of his hand.
Tori's left arm will follow.
Tori sinks down and then rises as if collecting his energy.
With a release of gathered energy, Tori turns counterclockwise at the waist and extends out over Uke's head.
Uke is thrown backwards with Kokyu Nage.

Kuden

In all Shomen Uchi techniques the Uke could use a weapon such as a club, knife or bottle.
The technique is even the same for a defense against a downward cut with the sword.
One must slide past Uke like two Japanese sliding doors.
Rather than extending the arm out it should be noted that one could strike with the elbow (the left in this case) for all Kokyu Nage techniques like this.

As Uke strike down slide past with the arms up and then turn around.

Tori steps forward and brings his arms down over Uke's arm.

*Tori rises and turns his hips couterclockwise
to throw Uke with Kokyu Nage.*

Another Variation

Uke comes forward with a front kick to Tori's
chest or stomach.
When Uke kicks, Tori moves back by shifting
his weight to his rear leg.
Contact is actually made between Uke's foot
and Tori's chest.
Tori catches the foot with both hands or with
one hand.
Tori will now surge forward throwing Uke
onto his back.

Zenpo Geri Kokyu Nage
The Breath Throw
Response to a Front Kick

Tori and Uke face each other in Hidari Ai Hanmi.

Uke steps forward and attempts to kick Tori in the stomach or chest with a front kick. Tori will step forward with his left foot and back with his right at a 45 degree angle facing slightly to the right to get off line of the attack.
At the same time, the incoming kick is caught from the inside and guided to the right hip. Tori will slide forward and extend his arms over Uke's chest and head throwing him with Kokyu Nage.

Kuden

By moving back a few inches by shifting your weight to you rear leg, the power of a front kick can be diffused.
Therefore, by shifting forward one is given even more distance when shifting back. Being only a few inches off is all that is necessary to potentially imbalance the adversary.

As his kick comes in it is though the energy
were inhaled by Tori.
Uke naturally feels as though he kicked
something that is now not there.
It is like leaning on a door that is not
completely closed and falling through the
doorway.
As Uke's foot is caught, he may think to pull
back and it is at this moment that he is
thrown with Kokyu Nage.
Breathe in the opponent and then breathe out
to throw him.
On one leg the adversary can easily be
knocked over.

Variation

Tori moves forward and to the outside of the
kick as described above.
This time however he will catch the kick from
below with both hands.
Tori's right palm will be under the foot and
the left hand under the calf.
When the power of the kick terminates, Tori
will turn his hips and shoulders to the left and
throw his arm up.
This throws Uke backward onto his back.

Tori and Uke face each other in Hidari Ai Hanmi.

Uke attempts a right front kick.

Tori catch the leg on the left hip and surges forwar.

Variation

Tori catches the kick from below.

Tori throws his arms up with a rocking motion.

Uke is thrown backwards.

Yoko Geri Kokyu Nage
The Breath Throw Response to a Side Kick

Tori and Uke face each other in Gyaku Hanmi.

Uke steps forward and attempts to kick Tori in the chest or stomach with a side kick.
Tori steps forward with the left foot then moves his right foot back so that he is not facing the right.
At the same time he scoops up Uke's kick from the outside and catches it in the bend of his elbow.
Tori will now step in and sweep Uke's left leg with his right foot.
The captured leg is thrown back towards Uke.
Uke is thrown to his back.

Kuden

Practice the very important timing in this technique.
This should be done in one spontaneous motion.

Mawashi Geri Kokyu Nage
The Breath Throw Response to a Round Kick

Tori and Uke face each other in Gyaku Hanmi.

Uke attempts to kick Tori in the left side with a round kick.
As the kick comes in Tori slides steps forward and to the right and catches the kick in the bend of his left elbow.
Tori turns his hips to the right and his shoulders turn as well.
This turns Uke's kick leg over so the back side of the leg is facing up.
Tori will strike down on the calf or thigh of Uke's right leg with a right hammering fist.
At the same time Tori pulls back.
Uke is jerked down face first.

Kuden

This can be very dangerous for Uke as he might suddenly fall on his face.
The front breakfall should be learned well before attempting this technique.

Chapter

11

Irimi Nage

Irimi Nage means "entering throw."
These techniques are characterized by a
bold entry.   Typically a slight angle

offline is used to come forward into the Uke's space. Often the Uke is turned or spun around only to be thrown to the ground on his back. Irimi Nage is perhaps one of the hardest techniques to learn and one should practice it well slowly and work up to an increased flow with rhythm and speed.

Katatate Irimi Nage
The Entering Throw Response to the Hand Being Seized

Tori and Uke face each other in Migi Ai Hanmi.

Uke steps forward and seizes Tori's right wrist with his left hand.
Tori will cross step forward with his left foot, move his right hand to the left and press the side of Uke's left elbow to his body.
Tori frees his right hand as his right foot goes forward deeply behind Uke.
Tori turns to face the same direction as Uke and lightly cups Uke's ear and moves his head to Tori's left shoulder.
Tori will now step back deeply with his left foot and lower his hips.

This will cause Uke to fall backwards and turn into an empty space.
Uke turns and comes up to regain his balance.
At this moment, Uke is thrown with Irimi Nage.

Kuden

To practice the feeling of how Uke should fall back, practice this with a partner.
Stand behind your partner and tilt one of his shoulders down.
Lightly pull both shoulders back so that your partner loses his balance.
Get out of the way because your partner will back-peddle looking for his balance until he suddenly turns around and then rises up again.
Only by turning around and rising will he find his balance.
It is at this moment and in this position that this Irimi Nage throw is made.
Repeat this until you can manipulate his balance well.
Uke should practice keeping his feet moving under his shoulders.
Failure to do this will certainly result in lack of stability.

Uke seizes the right hand.

Tori steps and presses Uke's elbow to his body.

*Tori steps, and turns as he brings Uke's head
to his left shoulder.*

Tori steps back and Uke falls backwards.

As Uke is spun around, he attempts to regain his balance. As he rises he is thrown down.

Kosadori Irimi Nage
The Entering Throw Response to a Cross Grab

Tori and Uke stand in Gyaku Hanmi.

Uke steps forward and seizes Tori opposite hand.
Tori turns his right hand and palm down and his hips to the right.
This has the effect of turning Uke's torso away to the side and exposing is backside.
Tori steps in with his left foot to Uke's rear right quandrant, and faces the same direction as Uke.
Tori will now place the base of his index finger and hand on Uke's neck just below the

ear (dokko den) with his left hand and gently move Uke's head to his right shoulder.
Tori's other arm can be extended out or may be down as shown.
Tori will now turn his hips and feet 180 degrees to the left.
Tori's right hand will rise and pass over Uke's chest and left shoulder.
This will cause Uke's back to arch and his head to go back to avoid being hit.
Tori will then step forward and extend his arms for the Irimi Nage.

Kuden

Uke's back must be arched and his head must be made to go back.
For young people this is easier.
For middle-aged people who have less flexibility in their spine, this may not be possible and may affect the usefulness of this technique.
Some people will try to turn away rather than arching their back.
This is dangerous as one should never turn away from a view of your opponent if possible.
Uke can be hit in the face with the bicep as the right arm throws him.

Uke seizes Tori's wrist.

Tori turns his hand and hips to the right.

Uke's head in brought to the right shoulder.

Tori turns his hips only and is in position to throw.

*Tori steps forward with his right foot and throws
with Irimi Nage.*

In the picture at the top of the page the
arm that is going across Uke's chest can
be doing a variety of things. If one
practices kindly with beginners, there is
no real contact being made. For real defense
purposes this could be a strike done with the
bicep as the arm goes form a bent position
and is straightened abruptly. The hand could
clip the chin or throat getting to this position.
One could also use an elbow or other hand
strike. These strikes in Japanese are called
atemi.

Ryotetori Irimi Nage
The Entering Throw
Response to Both Wrists
Being Seized

Tori and Uke face each other in Shizen Tai.

Uke seizes both of Tori's wrists.
As the wrists are just to be grabbed move the
left hand across to the side of the right arm
and pull the right hand back beyond Uke's
reach.
In this position Uke will not get a good hold
on either hand.
Use the edge of your left hand to cut across
and down in a clockwise semi-circle to the
outside of Uke's left arm.
This will move his whole body sideways.
Step forward with you leftt foot and then
behind Uke's leftt foot with the right foot so
that you are on Uke's left side.
Tori will then move Uke's head to the left
shoulder with the right hand on the neck.
Tori steps back with his left foot and lowers
his hips.
Tori has moved out of the way so Tori will
fall into this open space created by stepping
back.
This sends Uke falling backward .

Since his left shoulder in lower he will turn
around as he falls backwards.
As he rises to regain his balance, Tori will
throw with Irimi Nage.

Kuden

This is not a standard technique for doing
Irimi Nage.
However, one must be able to get to just
about any technique using the basics.
The cutting motion which turns Uke's body is
reminiscent of a motion used to flick the
blood of of a sword called *chiburi*.

Tori has cut across both of Uke's arm as he has
tried to seizes Tori's wrists. Tori enters to Uke's side.

Step back and when Uke rises follow his motion to throw him.

Extend your arm with the thumb down and step forward.

Extend out and maintain mindfulness (zanshin).

Katamune Tori Irimi Nage
The Entering Throw Response to a Chest Grab

Tori and Uke face each other in Gyaku Hanmi.

Uke steps forward and seizes Tori's left lapel with his right hand.
Tori turns his hips to the left and moves his right hand across past Uke's right arm.
Tori now moves his hips back to the right and his right goes under Uke's arm above the elbow.

This causes Uke's elbow to bend and Uke is locked up painfully.
Tori can now use strikes (atemi) or pressure points (kyusho) to the face.
Place the base of the left index finger just below the ear on the neck.
This point in a pressure point called *dokko*.
Tori then steps forward deeply behind Uke's right leg to throw him.
Uke's arm is still entangled and may break so proceed with caution.

Kuden

This employs the cutting motion described in the previous technique.
This motion should always be done in unison with the movements of the hips.
It cannot be done correctly with strength.

As Uke grabs the lapel strike with the hand sword (tekatana) to the his temple.

Reach over Uke's arm and then turn the hips back to bend and lock his arm.

*Place the right hand on his stomach and the left hand
on his neck below the ear. Step forward to throw.*

Munetsuki Irimi Nage
The Entering Throw
Response to a Chest Punch

Tori and Uke face each other in Hidari Ai
Hanmi.

Uke steps forward and punches to Tori's
chest or stomach with strong spirit.
Tori steps slightly to the left to get off line of
the attack and uses his left hand to parry the
attack to the side.

Tori then enters with the right foot to the rear
of Uke's right foot.
At the same time a counter attack is made to
Uke's face.
(See pictures for Yokomen Uchi Irimi Nage
as the strike to the face are the same.)
Uke is thrown to the ground as a result of the
simultaneous attack and entry.

Kuden

Do not only practice Irimi strikes one way.
The danger in this is that we fight the way we
train.
Your actions should be intentional and not an
automatic reaction.
Practice delivering atemi during practice as it
will train your eyes to see openings and
develop the timing necessary to exploit them.

Yokomen Uchi Irimi Nage
The Entering Throw Response to a Strike to the Side of the Head

Tori and Uke stand facing each other in
Hidari Ai Hanmi.

Uke steps forward with his right foot and strikes to the left side of Tori's head with his right hand.

Tori enters in directly by jamming Uke's right arm as it is pulled up and back to strike in.

Tori presses in with the edge of his hand or forearm into Uke's right inner arm.

This stops has attack from the onset.

Tori then steps forward with his right foot behind Uke's right foot and at the same time will either do Irimi Nage as shown in previous techniques or will strike the face with the palm or fist.

Uke falls to his back.

Kuden

This is not done with a one, two, three count. The movements blend into one continuous movement.

Tori jams up the right arm and enters with an elbow to the chin.

Tori jams the strike and uses the heel of the palm to Uke's face.

Shomen Uchi Irimi Nage
The Entering Throw Response to a Strike to the Head

Tori and Uke face each other in Gyaku Hanmi.

Uke steps forward with his right foot and strike down towards Tori's forehead with a right open hand strike or with a weapon.
Toril will step forward with his left foot and raise his hands up to create a triangular wedge to protect his from the strike.
This movement forward and off line gets Tori out of the way.
Tori will pivot and turn around guiding Uke's attacking hand down with his right hand.
Tori places his left hand on Uke's neck or cup his ear and brings it to his right shoulder.
Tori will step back with his right foot and lowers his hips.
Uke falls backwards but his shoulders are not level so he turns himself and tries to regain his balance.
Just before he rises enough to regain his balance he is thrown with Irimi Nage.

Kuden

Most of the problems with Irimi Nage come from these problems.

If Uke strikes down and you are applying any counter tension to his arms, his motion will stop.
The solution is to slide by Uke.

If you are grabby and try to man-handle Uke's neck, he will resist.
The solution is to guide and not force so keep a light yet firm touch.

If you don't get out of the way, Uke doesn't have a space to fall into.
The solution is to get out of the way.

If Uke is running into your arm extended out to the side like a clothesline you are not doing it right.
The solution is to keep your throwing arm in front of you and not let it go out to your side. You will accomplish this by moving your body in relation to your arms correct position.

Practice this slowly step by step over and over again.

If you are doing it correctly your Uke will feel like he has been caught up in a whirlpool.
If your Uke feels like a pinball, it needs more work.

Tori slides past Uke's downward strike.

Tori brings Uke's head to his right shoulder.

Tori steps back with his right foot and Uke will continue coming
forward to regain his balance. In this picture he has not turned and
come around yet.

Uke will step forward and with his right foot and throw
Uke with Irimi.

Zenpo Geri Irimi Nage
The Entering Throw Respnse to a Front Kick

Tori and Uke face each other in Shizen Tai.

Uke comes forward with a front kick to Tori's chest or stomach.
As the kick comes in Tori turns his hips to the left dramatically as though turning his back to the kick.
He then turn his hips back again to the right. As Tori does this he is actually moving his body off and then back on the line of attack. As a result the kick misses him and since this happens quickly, his behind spins Uke's body and causes Uke is lose his balance and at times even his footing.
Tori keeps his right hand up and it is in a position to throw Uke with Irimi Nage.

Kuden

When kicking, the body's musculature and nervous system has the expectation of hitting a target.

That target is judged mentally as having a
certain weight, distance, density etc...
When the kick passes through the air and
misses it is a shock as these exectations are
not met, and the brain must recalibrate
everything in order to sustain balance.
This is why attacks done at full speed and
without any restraint are extremely dangerous
for the person attacking.
This is especially true when Aiki principles are
used because the force that the attacker brings
to the table will be used against him.
With that said, Uke should really kick hard
and without reservations because this will
cause this technique to work even better.

Yoko Geri Irimi Nage
The Entering Response to a Side Kick

Tori and Uke face each other in Gyaku
Hanmi.

Uke steps forward and attempts to kick Tori
in the chest or stomach with a side kick.
Tori will make a sliding step back with first
the left foot and then the right foot.
This will cause Uke's kick to fall short of its
target.

As Uke's leg comes down from the kick, Tori
leaps with his left foot behind Uke and then
the right foot follows.
At this point Tori is behind Uke.
Tori seizes both of Uke's shoulders and pulls
back and down.
Uke falls to his back.

Kuden

In this technique Tori will in one jump twist
and pull Uke to the ground.
Practice leaping until this can be done
smoothly.

Variation

Uke attempts to kick Tori in the chest or
stomach with a side kick.
Slide step back and cross the hands blocking
the kicks with what is called an X-Block.
Use the left hand to rotate the foot so Uke's
leg turns over and his knee is facing down.
Surge forward to cause Uke to go face first to
the ground.

Step back and Uke's leg comes down.

Leap behind Uke and grab his shoulders.

Step back with the left.and pull Uke back.

Uke is thrown down on his back.

Chapter

12

Advanced Techniques

A t this level one should have the ability to flow easily from one technique to another and be able to use all eight basic techniques against the attacks presented in this book. You will become the most skilled at the techniques that you practice the most often. If you practice these techniques over and over again you will see that they keep teaching you new information. They are source in and of themselves of inspiration. Practicing with different partners will alert you to the differences among people and the adaptations that you will need to make for these techniques to work on all types of people. Aiki is about feeling and one technique does not express itself exactly the same on every person.

The advanced techniques were placed in this section because they are more difficult. Some of them may look easy but each one presents itself with different challenges. Other attacks are included in this section that were not previously discussed. At this level one should be able to start doing *ju waza* which means having several attackers come at you one at a time. In this exercise you can give a nod to the person you would like t to attack next. This exercise will help you to develop continuity. You may also enjoy practice *randori*. This is when you have multiple attackers come at you continuously with the same or different attacks.

Tenchi Nage
The Heaven and Earth Throw

Tori and Uke face each other in Shizen Tai.

Tori's right side is forward.
Uke steps forward and seizes both of Tori's wrists.
Tori will step back and to the right with his right leg.
Tori yields when grabbed and as he is grabbed Uke comes forward naturally at Tori's left side.

Tori will be firmly positioned and centered as
he lowers his right hand and raises his left.
Uke's forward energy is split up and down.
His feet feel like going forward and his head
feel like going back.
Uke falls on his back.

Kuden

This can be done statically but this would
involve being able to rotate the palm left palm
correctly in a spiraling motion to raise Uke'
right elbow.
To do this let the Uke grab your wrists with
your palms turned up, keeping the elbows
close to one's sides and then making a spiral
with the right hand downwards and the left
hand upwards.
Done with motion one feels as though one is
diffusing Uke forward momentum by splitting
in between heaven and earth.
Point the index fingers towards heaven and
earth.
Don't push forward into the opponent's
energy.
By yielding to the motion you will not meet
resistance.
One can think of Tenchi Nage as two
separate techniques in one.
The up or heaven side can throw an
opponent and the down or earth side can
throw an opponent.

If you meet resistance on the heaven side then bend your knees to drop the opponent using the earth side.

If the opponent gives you resistance on the earth side then throw him from the heaven side.

Uke seizes both of Tori's hands.

At the moment Uke is thrown Uke right leg comes forward and Uke could be hit in the face by Tori's knee.
This creates an impetus for Uke to go into a roll.

Variation

When Uke's wrist is grabbed, Tori will rotate his right hand blade (tekatana) counterclockwise around Uke's right hand as he steps back to draw Uke forward.
Tori moves his right hand into place so that Uke's wrist is in the web between his right thumb and index finger.
Tori may strike to Uke's face (atemi) with the left hand.
Tori cuts down at Uke's neck while raising Uke's right hand vertically.
Tori steps forward with the right leg and throws.
(See variation's pictures)

Step forward and to the right and strike Uke.

Step forward with the left foot going under tha arm.

*Keep the arm vertical and the head down.
Project Uke into a throw.*

Variation

Uke seizes the wrist.

Step back.

Raise the arm and cut down at the neck

Project Uke outward with Kaiten Nage.

Gyaku Hiji Nage
Elbow Reversal Throw

Tori and Uke face each other in Migi Ai Hanmi.

Uke steps forward and seizes Tori's right wrist with his right hand.
Tori cut out to the side with the edge of his hand (tekatana) like sword turning Uke's shoulders.
Tori steps forward with his left foot to the outside and next to Uke's right foot.
Tori then pivots, turns and steps back with the right foot to face the same direction as Uke.
As Tori makes the left step forward he will bring his left arm deeply under Uke's right arm.
Uke's right hand will be brought near to Tori's right hip.
Tori slide steps forward and to the left throwing Uke at an angle.

Kuden

Uke is thrown slightly forward and to the left at an angle.
Tori brings Uke's right arm into hyper-extension as he is moving.
This causes Uke to rise to his toes and step forward into a roll as he is projected.

Uke steps forward and seizes the right wrist.

Tori cuts with his hand sword out to the side.

Tori brings arm up under Uke's right arm.

Project Uke forward into a throw.

Throw and maintain zanshin.

Koshi Nage
Hip Throw

This throw can be done against a cross grab (kosa dori) as shown but can also be done against a strike to the side of the head (yokomen uchi).

Tori and Uke face each other in Gyaku Hanmi.
Uke steps forward and seizes Tori's right hand with his right hand.
Tori will cut to the right with his hand sword to turn Uke's shoulders and present an opening.
Tori steps forward with the left foot in between Uke's legs and at the same time Tori brings his left arm up between Uke's legs.
Tori hold Uke's hand so that his wrist is bent.
Uke's arm is hyperextended over Tori's back.
Tori will lift Uke using his legs and throw him over his back and hips.
As Tori does this he will will lift with his left arm and pull down with his right arm.

Kuden

If Uke holds onto Tori and tucks his head, he will land on the ground safely.
If Uke tries to save himself in mid-air he is likely to fall on his head and be injured.

Uke should let Tori do this throw very slowly and learn to take the fall easily.
This is not a hard fall to take although it doesn't look that way.

Uke seizes Tori's right hand.

Tori seizes Uke's hand and goes between his legs.

Tori loads Uke by lifting with his knees.

Uke is thrown over and Tori will maintain the hold.

Variation

Tori reaises Uke's arm enters and pulls the arm forward.

Uke is thrown over the hips and low back .

Uke tucks his head in and falls safely.

When throwing as shown in this variation it is important that Uke fall over Tori. Tori is not lifting Uke up. This requires that Uke's seized arm is forward far enough that Uke falls forward over the top of Tori. Some people like to throw by leaning to the rear leg and then shifting the weight to the forward leg while throwing. This is another variation and requires that Tori turn to the front before throwing rather than being bent to the side. That variation however is harder on the knees and therefore may cause one to lose one's balance more easily.

Oguruma Nage
Wheel Throw

If Tori steps forward to grab or punch, intercept his wrist the right hand and his elbow with the left hand.
Tori puts his left fingers in the bend of the elbow.
Tori bends his elbow by bring his hand over Uke's right shoulder.
Tori will bend Uke's wrist as he does this and step forward with the right foot.
Uke's balance is broken and he leans to his right rear quadrant.
As Tori steps his elbow his Uke in the jaw.

As Uke continues to turn his hips, Uke falls on his back.

Kuden

Don't grab the wrist tightly.
Use your thumb and one finger (index or little finger) to hook the hand where is joins the wrist.
This is called *Tsuribari Kuden*.
By pressing the hand towards the body when bent will cause extreme pain.
The application as of this method is employed here in a technique.
In Daito Ryu the fifth basic pin called *Gokajo*.

As Uke grabs or punche you can seize his wrist and elbow as shown.

Fold Uke's arm at the elbow and brig his right hand
back over his right shoulder..
Your elbow will hit him in the jaw as you step forward.

Variation

Rather than turning the hips and stepping
forward with the right foot to enter in behind

Uke as in the previous technique, one can step behind Uke's right foot with the left foot and compress his wrist with both hands as shown against your body. This will get Uke up on his toes to relieve the pain if you are doing this correctly.

Fukuto
Inside of the Knee

Tori and Uke face each other in Shizen Tai.

Uke steps forward and seizes both of Tori's wrists.
Tori presents his palms towards Uke as he is grabbed.
Tori projects his index fingers and reaches up to seize Uke's wrist as though applying Yankyo to both arms.
Uke rises to his toes from the pain.
He applies pain with both index fingers to Uke's radius bones and then suddenly cuts out and down to both sides.
This causes Uke to stumble forward to his knees in front of Uke.

Kuden

The name Fukuto refers to the inside of the knees.
As Uke falls forward Tori could place Uke's head between his knees.
Uke's head would be locked this way while he holds Uke's arms out to the sides.
In the pictures I've chosen to strike Uke's face with the knee.

Uke seizes Tori's hands.

Tori applies a Yonkyo grip to both arms bringing Uke up on his toes.

Tori swiftly brings both arms out to the sides.

*Tori hits Uke in the head with his knee and
Uke falls back.*

Variation against a Push

*Keep your hand up as someone walk towards you.
Here the Uke tries to push with his right hand and
Tori has seized his fingers.*

Another View

Seize the fingers.

Bring Uke's fingers in a clockwise arc.

*Bring Uke's hand to your center as if to hold it like
a cup of sake or you may take Sankyo.*

Nikajo Gatame
The Seond Pin Entrapment

This could be used against a sleeve grab (*sode tori*) or a chest punch (*munetsuki*).

Tori and Uke face each other in Gyaku Hanmi.

Uke steps forward with his right foot and attempts to punch Tori in the chest or stomach.
Tori slide steps forward and to the left with his left foot to get off line and at the same time sweep Uke's punching arm to the outside with the edge of his left hand (*tekatana*).
Tori will continue to move his left hand around Uke's right elbow trapping his arm.
Tori pivots and turns taking Uke to the ground.

Kuden

This should be done in one continuous motion.

Tori guides Uke's hand to the side when he punches.

Tori hooks the elbow and keeps it straight to lock it.

Another View

Entering in and moving the arm to the side.

Turn trapping the arm.

Ude Ori
Arm Break

This technique uses a variation of Nikajo meaning this is a pinning version of the technique Nikkyo.

Tori and Uke stand in Shizen Tai.
Uke steps forward and seizes Tori's sleeve at the right elbow.
Tori will cover the grabbing hand firmly to his side and then move his arm downward to the inside of Uke's arm.
This creates a painful jointlock on Uke's wrist.

Kuden

There are two variations of this.
The first is pictured first here and shows Uke's right hand cutting down vertically to wrench Uke's wrist.
The second is pictured next showing Tori moving his right arm horizontally across his body creating a shearing of Uke's wrist.
Both techniques require that Tori keep Uke's wrist close to the body.
This is the key.

Uke seizes Tori's right sleeve.

Tori covers the hand.

Tori rotates his right arm over the top of Uke's forearm
Keeping Uke's hand close to his side.

Tori cuts down vertically with his right arm
wrenching the wrist.

Variation

Uke seizes Tori's left sleeve.

As Uke grabs, Tori may step back and cover the grabbing hand.

Tori cuts across his body from left to right wrenching the wrist.

Makihiji
Wrapping the Elbow

Tori and Uke face each other in Migi Ai Hanmi.

Uke steps forward with his left foot and seizes Tori's right sleeve with his left hand.
As Tori is grabbed he steps back with his right foot and delivers a strike to Uke's face with a left fist.
Tori then steps forward with his right foot deeply to Uke's left rear quadrant.

At the same time, Tori will pass his right arm
straight forward over Uke's arm.
Tori scoops up Uke's left arm at the elbow
with a straight arm.
Uke's arm bends painfully at the elbow.

Kuden

Keep the arm straight while scooping up
Uke's arm.
It is natural to want to bend the arm, but use
your hips to make this technique work and
keep the right arm as straight as possible.
If this is done correctly it will be very painful
to the Uke and he will rise up to his toes.

Uke steps forward and seizes Tori's right sleeve.

Tori slides forward and scoops up Uke's arm at the elbow.

Tori straigtens his leg and wrenches the elbow.

*Uke's posture is broken and he
is immobilized.*

Morote Dori
The Wrist Being Seized
with Both Hands

Tori and Uke face each other Gyaku
Hanmi.

Uke steps forwards and seizes Tori's right
wrist with both hands.

Tori will step forward with his left foot
next to Uke's right foot and at the same

time rotate his right hand around the
outside of Uke's right hand.
Tori will pivot, turn clockwise and take
Ikkyo on Uke's right arm.

Kuden

If someone uses both hands to grab you,
the person can easily be struck.
Therefore, this is a poor attack.
The movement of the seized arm is more
limited because of the strength used by the
opponent.
Keep in my mind that you can always move
your body even though you may not be
able to move your arm.

Ushiro Ryotetori Sankyo
The Third Lesson
Response to Both Hands Being Seized from Behind

There are two versions of this technique
that are commonly practiced. The first is a
static technique in which the Uke enters
from behind and seizes both of Tori's

wrists. In the second variation, Uke approaches Tori from the front and goes behind him to take his wrists. This variation is more dynamic. Both techniques are similar but the main difference is the static techniques is more linear whereas the other is more circular.

Version 1

Tori stands in Hidari Shizen Tai.
Uke walks up from behind and seizes both of Tori's wrists.
Tori will rotate his forearms inwards with internal rotation.
This causes Uke's elbows to rise and also makes it difficult to establish a firm grip.
Tori will then slide his right foot back and to the right while at the same time seizing the outside edge of Uke's right hand.
Tori slides under Uke's right arm being careful to stay close to his body.
Once Tori has passed under the arm, he frees his right hand and uses it to clamp onto Uke's fingers and apply torsion along with the other grab on Uke's wrist.
Finish by taking Uke down and immobilizing him as previously described in other techniques.

Version 2

Tori and Uke face other a further distance
as this is a dynamic rather than static
technique.
Tori stands in Migi Ai Hanmi.

Uke briskly runs towards Tori seizing his
right hand with his righ thand and then
makes his way behind Tori to seize his
other hand.
As Uke makes his way around Tori, Tori
will shift to the rear and right going under
Uke's right arm as before.
The rest is the same as Variation 1.

Kuden

Practice the static version until one is
proficient and then the dynamic variation
will easily fall in place for you.
In reality, once you behind you an attacker
may punch, grab or choke you.
You can do Ikkyo, Nikkyo, and Yonkyo
using the same entry.
It is best to never let anyone get behind
you.
One should naturally think of striking the
attacker with the left elbow if he were to
actually grab the hand and come around
you from behind as described.

Uke cross grabs the right hand.

As Uke goes around, Tori slips under Uke's right arm.

Take Sankyo on Uke's right hand.

Ushiro Ryokata Dori Yonkyo
The Fourth Lesson Response to Both Shoulders Being Seized from Behind

Tori stands in Shizen Tai and Uke steps up from behind and seizes Tori's clothing at the sides of the shoulders with both hands. Tori will seize Uke's right hand as shown in the picture below with his left hand as he

slides back and to the right with his right
foot.
Once under the arm, Tori continues to turn
counterclockwise until the hand can be
removed from the cloth.
Then Tori will take the Yonkyo with both
hands.

Kuden

Slip under Uke's arm staying close to him
and get far enough to the rear so that you
have enough space to take Yonkyo forward
in the direction Uke is facing.

Go under the arm and slide past Uke.

Take Yonkyo on Uke's right forearm.

Mae Kami Dori
The Hair Seized From the Front

Uke seizes Tori's hair from the front. with his right hand.
Tori steps forward with his right foot and compresses the sides of Uke's hand with both hands.
Tori then bends forward at the waist and Uke's wrist is wrenched.
Turn the hand over and apply the Nikkyo in which the wrist is flexed at a 90 degree angle.

Kuden

Compressing the bones of the hand will make it hard for Uke to maintain a grip.

Compress the hand, bend forward and then transition to Nikkyo.

Ushiro Kami Dori
The Hair Seized from the Rear

Uke walks up from behind and seizes Tori's hair with his right hand.
Tori immediately covers the back of Uke's hand with his left palm.
Tori turns clockwise and steps out with the left foot.
As Tori turns around Uke's wrist is twisted as in Kotegaeshi.

Kuden

Use your thumb nail to dig into the web on skin between the fingers.

Uke covers the grabbing hand.

Tori turns around and twists the wrist.

Ryomune Dori Kokyu Nage
The BreathThrowResponse to Both Lapels Being Seized

Uke runs towards Tori to seize both of his lapels.

As Uke gets close, Tori raises Uke's left elbow up with his right palm and presses in and down with his left hand at Uke's right elbow. At the same time Tori will step forward and to the right with his right foot to slide past Uke and get off line.

Tori will pivot and turn.
Uke continues to come forward with head
and torso leading.
Tori moves Uke past him by moving Uke's
left elbow forward with power from his right
leg and hip.
Uke is thrown forward.

Kuden

Slide past Uke like a sliding door.
Don't stop Uke's energy coming forward.

Slide past Uke and turn.

Uke is thrown forward with Kokyu.

Hiji Dori
Seizing the Elbow

Tori and Uke face each other in Shizen Tai.

Tori walks up to Uke and seizes his right
forearm just above the wrist with his right
hand.
Tori steps to the rear of Uke's right foot
with his left foot.
Tori pivots and turns to face the same
directions Uke while at the same time he
brings his left arm over the top of Uke's
right elbow.
Tori pulls down on Uke's wrist and raises
up on the elbow at the same time.
This causes Uke's fully extended elbow to
by hyperextended.

Tori can now suddenly turn his hips counterclockwise and drop to his right knee.
Uke is thrown over Tori's left knee behind Tori.

Kuden

This technique could be adjusted to use against a cross wrist grab or a right punch to the chest.
In this case the technique is an arresting technique.
Most people who have difficulty with this are trying to pull up on the elbow too much rather than pulling the hand down and getting the forearm into a vertical position.
If the hand is pulled down Uke will rise to his toes and arch his back because of the discomfort.

Tori seizes Uke's right wrist and turns it to the side.

Tori steps in and locks the elbow.

Guinomi Kuden
The Oral Transmission of the Sake Cup

This refers to how the hand is held in variations of Sankyo.
When the fingers are gripped tightly they are brought to one's center and resemble someone sipping *sake*.

This is an example of an arrest or come-along technique.

Tori approaches Uke and seizes his fingers of that his palm is one the backside of the fingers.

Tori will compress the fingers tightly and and then turn Uke's hand over to the inner side of the forearm is facing up.

Tori may then get Uke's cooperation as Uke rises to his toes.

Tori may also raise Uke's hand up and then extend out for a projection throw.

Kuden

Take the left side before the right because most people who are married will be wearing a ring which will add to the pain of the fingers being compressed.

Hold a cup without a handle and notice how the index finger wraps around the top of the cup.

This way of grasping the hand and bringing it upward towards the chest or face as if to take a sip of sake is where this gets its name.

Tori seizes Uke's fingers tightly and raises the wrist.

Extend Uke'shand forward and then make a large arc to project the Uke.

Kote Hineri
Twisting the Wrist

Tori and Uke face each other in Shizen Tai.

Tori walks up to Uke and seizes his right hand.
This could be done from a handshake.
Tori steps forward with his right foot to the outside of Uke's right foot.
Tori continues to turn counterclockwise so that Uke's right hand is twisted like a Kotegaeshi.
As Tori is about to turn all the way around to face Uke he uses the other hand to reinforce the hold.
Tori continues stepping in the direction of Uke's right rear quandrant.
Uke is thrown and Tori pursues Uke.
Uke is restrained face down with right arm vertical and the wrist compressed by both hands at a 90 degree angle.

Kuden

This throw is made by the continous turning
of the body.
You must turn completely around to
sufficiently bend Uke's wrist enough to take
him down.

Variation

If Uke cross grabs the wrist this technique
could also be done.

Tori seizes Uke's right hand.

Tori turns around twisting Uke's wrist.

Uke falls much like he does Kotegaeshi.

Atama Dori
Taking the Head

Tori and Uke face each other in Migi Ai Hanmi.

Tori steps deeply behind Uke's right leg and seizes Uke's right hand with his right hand at the same time.
Tori's right hand enters across Uke's neck and extends over his left shoulder.
Tori's immediate entry imbalances Uke and throws him backwards.

Kuden

This technique is sort of a combination of Irimi Nage and Kokyu Nage combined.
The Uke should fall with one swirft entry.
The throw is made by Tori stepping so far into Uke's space that he cannot maintain his balance when his head is forced to go back by Tori's arm being extended.

Variation

Rather than throwing Uke with a powerful
entry forward, Tori may turn his hips
counterclockwise to the left.
At the same time he will bend his left elbow
and capture Uke's head in his armpit.
The right hand still holds Uke's right wrist.
As a result of this hold Uke's back is arched
and he is basically supported by Tori.
At this point Uke could be taken along in
custody or simply dorpped.
Uke could be dropped on Tori's bent knee if
he steps back and kneels.
This of course would injury Uke's back.
Tori could also be dropped by stepping back
with the left foot and letting go of the head.
As Uke falls back, his elbow breaks on Tori's
thigh.
Tori slides the arm down his leg and uses the
shin as a fulcrum to flip Uke over on his
stomach.

Tori turns Uke's hand to the side so that he may enter.

From this position Uke can be thrown to his left side or Tori may seize Uke's head with his left arm.

Chapter

13

Illustrated
Concepts

This section of the book will deal strictly with concepts that should be studied to improve one's understanding of the mechanics of the techniques of Aiki Goshin Ho.   The ideas presented here may be understood logically by the beginning student, but only after training for a long time will they develop a deeper understanding of these principles.   This chapter was set up as a constant reminder to apply these principles in all techniques. I would say that the prinicples are more important than the techniques themselves. From these principles one is eventually able to see martial arts techniques develop freely as a creative process (takamusu aiki).

The picture below represents a directional force applied against an obstacle represented by a line line. The force is coming in at a right angle. In such a case it is the strength of the force versus the strength of the obstacle. If the force is greater then the line will be break, deform or be moved. If the line is stronger the arrow which represents force will be broken, deformed or be moved. Force is equal to the mass of an object multiplied by its acceleration. Therefore, if we apply this to the dynamics of an attack, we could increase the force we use by either increasing our size which is relative to mass or we could increase the speed. One may not be able to change one's mass. For the most part we have limited ability to change our mass. Speed declines with age and so these are attributes one should not depend on. This is not how we deal with an incoming force in Aiki Goshin Ho.

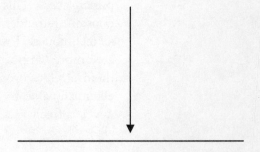

This illustration represents on another level how many people function in everyday life with conflict. When obstacles appear some people butt heads to get their way. Sometimes it works but at the expense of others. Sometimes it only serves to frustrate them. The techniques that are practiced in Budo (martial arts) should reflect the principles used to live one's life. One should be reflected by the other.

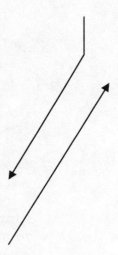

The diagram about illustrates some important concept used in Aiki Goshin Ho. The directional lines represent the force generated by an attack or body motion. Rather than being a stationary line that is fixed in space. A new arrow is shown which represents a new force which redirects the oncoming force by using a forward entry and a slight angle.

In this way the oncoming line is redirected and force against force is avoided. This can be applied to verbal conflicts as well as physical conflicts.

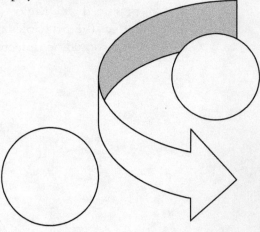

Faced with an arc of force coming at you, one cannot stay in place. The target of the force was chosen before the action began. Changing the location will cause the force to miss its target. In the diagram above a commonly used Aiki principle of going inside the arc of the force is shown. Becoming the axis of rotation is employed for such techniques as Irimi Nage or Kotegaeshi. Since the Uke travels along the cricumference of a larger arc the distance is longer and therefore generates more movement. Another possibility is to move back so that the arc passes in front of you.

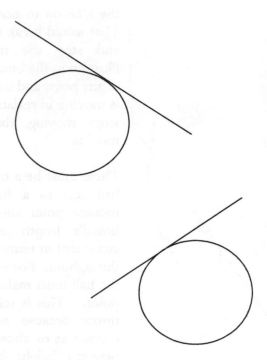

Arcs, circles and spirals are common in Aiki techniques. We tend to think of these shapes only happening in the horizontal plane. However, they occur vertically also and at diagonals, too. The illustration above demonstrates how a flat board would fall over a ball. If the ball moves, the board tips over. This principle is demonstrated in techniques like Koshi Nage in which the opponent is thrown over the hips. To

attacker it is used generally to produce a pain response so that we can control the person and immobilize him. Producing a pain response only may make the person "jumpy" and harder to manage so it is best not to rely on joint locks that produce pain only. One joint lock can flow into another. Ideally, joint locks are best applied when the person is held lightly and pulls or pushes thereby putting the lock on himself. This takes a lot of finesse that can only be acquired by long practice and good instruction. We will take a closer look at how joint locks are actually put together. All joint locks use leverage. The leverage that is used is either provided by Tori, or it is applied to Uke's joint using Uke's body to structurally apply leverage to his joints.

There are three basic parts of any lever. The first is the <u>fulcrum</u>. This is the part of a lever that allows rotation or movement around it. A fulcrum on a see-saw is in the middle. Both ends go up or down over this fixed point. For our purposes the fulcrum will be a fixed point in which can vary in location. Next is the <u>input force</u>. This represents the effort or strength applied to do some work. This force is supplied by the Tori as he attempts to take a joint lock on Uke. If the force applied is used to move something then what is moved is called a <u>load</u>. For our purposes we will refer to an opposing force to the load and call it the <u>output force</u>. The output force on a see-saw is the lifting up of the person sitting on it. The load, being in the opposite direction, is the purpose sitting.

First Class Levers

As you can see from the picture, the First Class Lever has the fulcrum between the input and output force. That means it is between the effort and the load. Let's take a look at how this is applied in real life. We have already talked about the see-saw. This is an example of a First Class Lever. Long ago when there were wagons that got stuck in the mud, people used lever so get the wheels out. A rock was put close to the wheel (fulcrum), and a board or strong branch was laid over the rock but under the edge of the wheel. As one pushes down on the free end, the fulcrum caused the board to lift the wheel up and out of the mud. Examples of how first class levers are used can be seen in the Seoi Nage, and Hiji Dori to name a few.

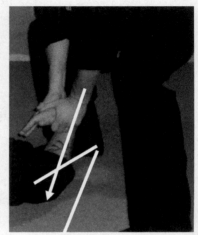

This an example of a Second Class Lever. Notice that the fulcrum represented by the circle is fixed, The input force is on the other end. The output force is in the wrist itself.

Second Class Levers

Here we can obviously see that there is painful compression of Uke's bent wrist. Tori is pushing down on the knuckles. This is the <u>input force that is on the end</u>. Uke's elbow is stable and pinned to the ground. This is the <u>fulcrum on the other end</u>. The <u>output force is in the middle</u> where the wrist breaks. An example of a second class lever would be seen in a wheelbarrow. Since the joint cannot move at the output force, the joint itself will be compromised and eventually the wrist will fracture. Because one can change the angle of the forearm on the ground without moving the elbow, the joint lock can be made more or less effective by getting the right angle. Many people will try to push down on the wrist itself, but this is incorrect. The farther away from the wrist (i.e. knuckles), the more intense the pain will be. As this angle becomes more acute, so does the pain

Third Class Levers

In a Third Class Lever the <u>fulcrum is on the end</u>. The <u>input force is in the middle</u> and the <u>output force is on the other end</u>. This is

commonly seen when one uses a broom. The picture demonstrates how force applied to the elbow has the effect of moving the Uke (the load) forward. This is also seen in techniques like Gyaku Hiji Dori.

Sometimes when students have problems usnderstanding how to make a technique work I explain the mechanics using levers. In some cases, students will mimic what they think they see and although the placement and position of the body may be correct, the use of force and the location of a fulcrum could be totally wrong. In other words, it is not uncommon for students to inappropriately use force at the wrong location.

About the Author

Dr. Clum is the founder of Aiki Goshin Ho Jujutsu. In addition to studying and teaching martial arts he is also a licensed Chiropractor, teacher, writer and artist. He teaches at the Azusa Bujinkan Dojo which he owns and operates. He produced Aiki Goshin Ho to preserve in his own practice and to pass on to others the most effective and essential techniques that he has learned from Aikido, Hapkido and Jujutsu. This is a process that has taken 30 years. He believes that each martial artist will come up with their own synthesis that is unique to themselves over time. This comes about as a natural expression of study, training, and experience. As of 2009, Dr. Clum holds the following ranks.

Aiki Goshin Ho, Founder
Bujinkan Budo Taijutsu, 5th Degree Black Belt, Shidoshi
AFJ Jujitsu-4th Degree Black Belt, Instructor
Yoshin Ryu Jujitsu-3rd DegreeBlack Belt
Hapkido-3rd Degree Black Belt
Aikido-1st Degree Black Belt

If you are interested in learning more about
Aiki Goshin Ho
Email me jamesnmichelle8@verizon.net

Azusa Bujinkan Dojo
www.azusabujinkan.com